"Brokenness is part of our humanity and Sarah Perry gets it. *Sand in My Sandwich* is her story of living with transparency, grace, humor, and hope. Wife, mom, attorney, writer, Sarah is every woman. No matter your challenge today, you will find yourself in her story. This book is a must-read for every woman and the man who loves her."

—**Shannon Royce**, president and CEO, ChosenFamilies.org

SAND in MY SANDWICH

SAND in MY SANDWICH

AND OTHER MOTHERHOOD MESSES
I'M LEARNING TO LOVE

SARAH PARSHALL PERRY

Revell

a division of Baker Publishing Group
Grand Rapids, Michigan

Published by Revell
a division of Baker Publishing Group
P.O. Box 6287, Grand Rapids, MI 49516-6287
www.revellbooks.com

Printed in the United States of America

Library of Congress Cataloging-in-Publication Data is on file at the Library of Congress, Washington, DC.

ISBN 978-0-8007-2410-8

Unless otherwise indicated, Scripture quotations are from the Holy Bible, New International Version®. NIV®. Copyright © 1973, 1978, 1984, 2011 by Biblica, Inc.™ Used by permission of Zondervan. All rights reserved worldwide. www.zondervan.com

Scripture quotations labeled ESV are from The Holy Bible, English Standard Version® (ESV®), copyright © 2001 by Crossway, a publishing ministry of Good News Publishers. Used by permission. All rights reserved. ESV Text Edition: 2007

Scripture quotations labeled NLT are from the Holy Bible, New Living Translation, copyright © 1996, 2004, 2007, 2013 by Tyndale House Foundation. Used by permission of Tyndale House Publishers, Inc., Carol Stream, Illinois 60188. All rights reserved.

Author is represented by WordServe Literary, Inc., www.wordserveliterary.com

15   16   17   18   19   20   21   7   6   5   4   3   2   1

For Noah, Grace, and Jesse,
who make the very best messes.

And for Matthew,
who reminded me it was always possible.

Contents

Acknowledgments

I extend my deepest gratitude to Lonnie Hull DuPont, who turned editing into the highest of art forms, and who was patient with someone for whom things sounded better in her head than they did on paper and had a predilection for inappropriate comma usage. I also want to thank Twila Bennett and Lindsay Davis for approaching marketing with the kind of fervor that an author knows will result in the dissemination of her passionately held message. I also want to thank my parents, Craig and Janet Parshall, who have weathered their own challenges with aplomb, perseverance, and an unwavering faith that the best is yet to come. I am also thankful to my friends and extended family for whom "You should really write a book about this" was a recurrent theme in our conversations, Revell Books for believing I was a viable literary risk, and my agent Alice Crider for pushing a product in which she had confidence from the start.

I also want to thank my brood—Noah, Grace, and Jesse—who were living real life alongside my writing of it, and who were as tolerant as they could be when Mommy sequestered herself in the office. Every day in this life I am privileged to share with them is rife with material for multiple books and future embarrassment. I will undoubtedly be the mother at the rehearsal dinner regaling their future spouses with stories I'm sure they will prefer I not share. In that case, I will just hand out copies of this book. They love me miraculously. They are my great reward.

Final and greatest thanks go to my husband, Matt, who began this chaotic journey with me, and to whom I can say my only wish is that it all had started sooner.

1

The Beginning of the End

He lifted me out of the slimy pit,
    out of the mud and mire;
he set my feet on a rock
    and gave me a firm place to stand.

Psalm 40:2

I am not famous. I am just a mother, and a writer, and ordinary in about every way imaginable. I write most days in my pajamas facing a fine view out the second-story window of a sprawling, elegant property I do not own. That is actually part of this story: the story of a life, and a messy one at that.

Then? My life was neat and ordered and under control. Now? My life's a mess. Ask my friends.

Actually, don't. They won't see it through the veil of forced perfection. I am the one who still sometimes suppresses the urge to fly hysterically through the house with the Windex when I hear from my husband—the guy who doesn't believe in charades of any sort—that we're about to have houseguests. He will greet you at the door in his pajamas, sporting slippers with holes worn through to the floor, and hair of the most profound bed-head variety. I, however, have learned to course-correct with little more than an hour's notice, and by the time we open our door (if I am lucky), the floors might be swept and there is food on the counter. This food might be nothing more than a half bag of tortilla chips I've unearthed in our pantry, or a cup of questionably fresh mixed nuts. Please don't look in the closet. You're likely to be hit by the avalanche of unhung coats. And for the love of Pete, don't smell the carpets. The dogs are in some kind of territorial "pee-off."

Mine could be described as a typical mother's life: the life of a typical mother with a typical control problem, and a pretty swell grasp on how to "out-Jones" the Joneses. Think Stepford Wife with fewer mechanical gears; a wife and a mother who could never stand the mess.

Let me set the stage.

Imagine an ever-so-slightly uptight lawyer with vacuum lines in her carpet, an immaculate Toyota, and an apartment that smells of orchids. Her spice cabinet is arranged alphabetically. Her taxes are finished in January. Then, imagine a small-town hero with a giant Ford pickup, sheets he can't remember washing, and no college degree. Now, imagine a brief courtship, a hastily set wedding date, and the lawyer thinking to herself, "I can change him."

Don't ever, EVER think this about another person.

14

Once, when things were orderly, when I was a single girl with a singular fixation on controlling everything, I took a trip to Jerusalem and placed into a gap in the city's ancient Western Wall a folded note telling the Lord that I'd had enough of the incessant striving, the deep soul unrest that was keeping me awake at night. I told him I needed patience to wait for that right man, someone who, in my partnership with him, would nudge me closer to God. His response was something like, "You sure about this?" Six months later, the man with the blue pickup and a wild, impassioned faith showed up. He also had food on his shirt. To this day, the man ends up with as much on his clothes as he does in his mouth.

Matt and I bonded quickly and married within a year of meeting. This is where things stop sounding like a Nicholas Sparks novel. It was, in fact, the beginning of the end. It was the first step toward termination of a way of life to which I'd held fast for two decades.

It was very clever of God to use someone handsome to help get the job done.

In the first ten years of our marriage, Matt and I experienced trials that some people never see in a lifetime. Our theory was that the bond was made strong because the challenges would prove likewise formidable. The two of us? Well, we must have looked to everyone else like a sinking ship. And you have to be pretty committed to going down with the vessel to ignore the part of you that's fighting the urge to scan the deck for the life rafts. Yet from those crevices, those gaps of hardship between the quiet, prosperous periods, a precious and essential faith has sprung. *Essential* faith. Essential to my not making off in the Honda with a suitcase full of chick flicks and a bag of dirty laundry. Essential because our life is a mess. But then, God loves messed-up people.

In addition to a raft of deaths, illnesses, job losses, and financial devastations, we've had yet another series of trials to endure: those packaged neatly in the form of three tow-headed, blue-eyed, dimpled children. These are children who look as though they've fallen straight from a Michelangelo tableau. These are also children who enjoy locking both themselves and each other in the dogs' cages, partly because they find small spaces comforting and partly because they find it comforting to torture each other. They are both typical and extraordinary at the same time, a blessing and a challenge both, very much the accessories of any mother's life, but perhaps more uniquely so.

My oldest son Noah has Asperger's syndrome—a form of high-functioning autism. He is also a "puker." I used to think that his overactive gag reflex was simply a sensitivity we needed to cure. It appeared to us, the autism uninitiated, that he just had to toughen up a bit. But at many dinners, Noah insisted there was sand or "fuzz" or dog hair in his food. One small gag would lead to a giant mess in never enough time for me to fly across the kitchen and hurtle him into the bathroom. And Lord help us if we were dining out. How do you convince the poor teenage waiter with his jaw on the floor that "no, the cheeseburger is perfectly fine, but my son believes someone dropped it in a sandbox on the way to the table"?

On one such occasion, Noah was in the height of his foot aversion. If there was a naked foot—or even just a manicured toe—within arm's length of his dining chair, the end was near. My daughter Grace found this sensitivity to be highly propitious.

At lunch with their hot dogs one day, Grace was playing with her unshod Barbie doll at the table and Noah started to heave.

"Grace!" Noah screamed. "Get your Barbie *off the table!*"

I was at a loss for the particular cause of that day's retching.

"Noah, what is the problem with her Barbie? She's playing so nicely, honey."

"Mom!" (gag) "It's her feet!"

At which point Grace proceeded to dip her Barbie's naked feet in her puddle of ketchup, dreamily swirl them around, and lick the entire thing off.

Twenty minutes of clean-up thereafter commenced.

The other day, I pulled back the sheets on my bed and discovered what looked to be a large quantity of small colored pebbles. First response? Infuriation. I had to pick out every last one by hand. Panic struck me as I imagined our fish flopping on the bathroom floor—devoid of her water and aquarium gravel. I fumed thinking about how long it was going to take one of the kids to fess up to some weird, ritualistic fish sacrifice. Then curious, I put one in my mouth because, of course, that's the best way to determine what something is. The pebbles turned out to be rock candy, and they were delicious.

Messy and delightful. This, I have found, is pretty much what it's like to be a parent.

Attempting perfect control is impossible in an imperfect world. It's even more unattainable a goal in parenting, where we parents flail and lunge and trip toward raising decent children who love the Lord and sometimes eat their broccoli. There is no perfect family; there is no life free of mess. But God reminds us: "Your words have supported those who stumbled; you have strengthened faltering knees" (Job 4:4). And boy, do we stumble. In the midst of it all, He is there, reminding us, "My child, I got this."

The chaos of our lives has crafted an awareness in my life of where God is to be found. Spoiler alert: God is *not* in an immaculate house, hand-crafted baby announcements, or duck consommé. God is not in all the perfect things we naively think we need, or all the things we see perfectly staged in magazines about which we can later feel guilty because we don't have the time, money, or energy to accomplish them for ourselves. Don't misunderstand. I believe God loves beautiful things, but when one finally gets one's priorities in order, one realizes that polishing the silver for one's dinner party is overrated. If I may, let me suggest ordering a pizza and putting out some paper plates. I love Martha Stewart, but the woman probably hasn't held a baby in over four decades. I'm guessing she's got more time than I do to glue decoupage robin eggs on a wreath for Easter. I, however, am now totally content to stick a ceramic bunny on the kitchen counter and call it a day.

I thank God now (with hindsight I might once have chosen to do without) for the challenges that filled my life after marriage. I thank Him for willing that things become harder and require more of us, because the "untidying" of life was the only way I started truly looking for Him. When I did, He made Himself found, as He always does in the midst of disarray. One night while working in my office, a naked Jesse

18

walked in, screaming "Mail!" and delivered (read: dropped and scattered all over the floor) half the stack of paper I'd just bought, paper I needed to print what I was writing, among other things, about my kids who do things exactly like that.

What an untidy, ever-wise work in progress we are.

Matt and I have often asked ourselves, "In a million years, could you EVER have anticipated our lives would have turned out this way?"

The answer is no. No, we could not.

This is the story of how God used my children and my life's messes as instruments of His presence. It is a tale of how things had to fall apart before they could be put back together the right way. And I learned that, on this grand adventure, chaos looks a lot like perfect order in disguise.

2

Angst and the Type A

"For I know the plans I have for you," declares the Lord, "plans to prosper you and not to harm you, plans to give you hope and a future. Then you will call on me and come and pray to me, and I will listen to you. You will seek me and find me when you seek me with all your heart."

Jeremiah 29:11–13

The well from which I draw the material herein is deep and personal and with me every day. There is so much in this busted-up life to share that, even for a natural introvert like me, the easiest part of remembering my story is simply pulling from what's there—talking about me, and the people attached to me, and the kind of stuff that literally no one would believe if it happened to anyone else *but* me. I get a lot of that. "Only you, Sarah . . ."

In 1979, the famous memoirist Joan Didion wrote in the *New York Review of Books* that "self-absorption is general, as is self-doubt."[1] I am generally good at both. So you can just sit there and nod knowingly, and thank God you weren't dumb enough to take all your own general messiness and spew it out for someone else to laugh at. I'll take care of that for you. You're welcome.

But thinking about this nonlinear journey necessitates a discussion of the lessons learned: the ones that were hard-won and painful and that I am still learning every day, though I'd like to say I'm finished and on my way to a well-deserved vacation. I do, sometimes, think I'd be fairly happy with a holiday from my own life. I'd like to be past the hard parts, but that's not His plan. New lessons come to me as quickly as I reminisce about the old ones; even as I ruminate on the past, the present comes at me hard and fast, with more to overcome and to learn.

Hard too is the peeling back of whatever protective layers of anonymity still exist between me and the outside world. There've been some ridiculous goings-on in this fractured and fulfilling life of mine, and not all of them are easy to discuss. Some are, in fact, downright embarrassing. I guess I'm part of this new "culture of confession": those of a tribe that believe there is value in transparency—that the realities of flawed character and ugly struggle are to be esteemed because of the healing value they might have in someone else's life. I hold my treasure in a "jar of clay," to show that whatever power in me is not of *me*, but of *Him* (2 Cor. 4:7). If there's something to be said for where I am, it is that none of this journey has been in vain. He shows me every day what He is doing with these lessons and these children of mine. I am a woman blessed beyond measure.

My cup overflows. It just took me awhile to figure that out.

～

If you believe in the psychology of birth order, which I do and about which I know there are books written, though I haven't read any because I'm too busy with the life I'm about to lay out for you, you know that oldest children (as I am) are prone to overachievement and a heightened sense of responsibility. For most of my life, I've taken these traits and crafted them to a level of hypervigilance so that the average bystander might think I could alter the universe with my worrying. In fact, I believed it myself. I was told over a decade ago that my sympathetic nervous system (the one responsible for maintenance of fight-or-flight response) was in perpetual overdrive. A friend likened me to a prey animal whose eyes dart continuously, scanning the forest for the thing that might at any moment spring forth and eat her. This is fine if you're a rabbit and your brain is the size of a grape. When you're human, it downright sucks the life out of you.

How, then, did I come to such a state? Though I am the first of my parents' four children, did I emerge from the womb inherently driven? Was I always as maniacal as the Duke of Wellington, who once famously proclaimed, "I am obliged to be everywhere and if absent from any operation, something goes wrong. . . . Success can only be attained by attention to the most minute details"?[2] No. There was instead, as there is for all ways of being, a foundation upon which my psyche was built that made me the woman, the wife, and most critically, the mother I eventually became. It was on the early path of my life, as a young single woman, that my mind's fortress was built. Once laid out, it will become evident how very hard it was to be torn down. I am daily, and with God's mighty grace, still pulling out stones from the walls of this fortress.

My childhood was routine and happy. Suffice it to say that if a movie were made of my life, it would show a blonde girl with braids, running in slow motion with her basset hound puppy through long backyard grass to a jungle gym while something by Thomas Newman plays in the background. This is before she and her three siblings (a neat package of two girls and two boys in total) start pushing each other off said jungle gym.

There was a Barbie cake on my tenth birthday with a doll stuck right in the middle, and her ball gown dress made of vanilla sponge cake with pink icing. There was a two-week family vacation across the northwest into the Dakota Badlands, to Colorado, to Mount Rushmore, with all six of us crammed into a minivan, where my brother and I used the seam in the car upholstery as the "do not cross" line, because there is only so much of your twelve-year-old brother you can take when you're traveling in ten cubic feet of space. There were Big Wheel races down our street with my sister, Christmas in Wisconsin with three feet of snow on the ground, and a visit from the tooth fairy in kindergarten. There was my friend Mary who lived with her family across the alley from my house, and who had been adopted from India at the age of five. I loved her more than just about anything in the world. Except horses. I was stupid crazy about horses.

My parents adored us. They stood up for us, protected us, nurtured us, prayed for us. And that is beyond all the standard parental fare: you know, your basic feeding, clothing, vaccinating. But reality has a way of creeping in and a child can only be protected from the biological mechanisms of a decaying earth for so long. When I turned thirteen, my uncle—my mom's brother—was diagnosed with non-Hodgkin's lymphoma. Within nine months, my mother's other brother *and* her mother were both diagnosed with hairy cell leukemia. My mother was very nearly the age then that I am now. I remember a number of trips to the University of Chicago hospital. Someone was always in surgery. Someone was always in chemo or radiation. Not long after, my brother Sam contracted bacterial meningitis and had to be hospitalized for many days. It was the first time that I felt the footing under my feet begin to ripple with uncertainty and fear. I couldn't bear to be a burden to my parents when everything else had suddenly become so hard.

In high school, a new philosophy emerged. My internal metronome was no longer repeating only the "do, do, do" mantra of responsibility. Now it added the "be, be, be" of betterment and comparison. I looked around me at kids from all over the county and felt myself growing smaller with what I didn't have. It was as if someone sat me down and said, "Listen, kid, you're of average intelligence, passably good-looking, with a ho-hum physique and no real athletic ability. You've gotta distinguish yourself somehow. How about this: be the best at everything." So convinced was I of this new creed that I could not be persuaded otherwise. I stepped up my performance, my responsibility, my dependability. I was always on call, on hand, on edge. I listened for signs of distress and jumped into action, and I did it all while auditioning for the lead in the musical and driving volunteer projects through Future Leaders of America.

I was learning the art of circumstantial manipulation, and I was terribly good at it. I had developed a system to build the perfect machine: me.

Complicating things was my friend Jill. Jill (not her real name, though it should be because I'm about to dump a bunch of compliments on her and if she is reading this she will know exactly who "Jill" is, anyway) was the epitome of everything I wanted to be: tall, exotic, smart, talented. She had been in beauty pageants. She came from money. She danced ballet. I came from church and had done a jazz recital once where I dressed as a hobo, complete with knapsack, overalls, and coffee grounds stuck to my face with theater glue. A *hobo*.

Over time, our friendship became less about how cute we thought Jason Priestley was and more about how many times each of us had made the honor roll. This subterfuge was never directly spoken of, only implied. Because that is the way high school girls can be with one another: purposeful in their python stealth, never saying the things that are mutually understood, things that would have been inconceivable for one of us to say to the other, things like "I really like you as a friend, but I am super intimidated by you. So, I find myself competing with you for attention and to prove my worth." My strategy was to prove my quality to her and to everyone else the only way I knew how: do more and achieve more. I set as my goal the biggest "achievements" paragraph in the high school yearbook at the end of our senior year. By George, if I wasn't a National Merit

Scholar, I was going to look like a real team player on paper. Softball, cheerleading, prom committee, student council. I joined anything for which I demonstrated marginal capability, or that would take me on as a charity project.

By the end of the school year, my paragraph was over one inch thick. Exactly as thick as Jill's. Though hers had better stuff.

It was torture on my sympathetic nervous system.

She went on to graduate from Stanford University and is now a doctor practicing in California. So, I'm pretty sure I lost.

~

College began at a Big Ten university in the Midwest. It ended at a small Christian college in the South. The transfer there is still the subject of an ongoing "disagreement" between my parents and me, as the two experiences couldn't have been more different. I told them I was just fine where I was, thank you very much. I went from singing the lead of Sally Bowles in *Cabaret*, to getting busted by my resident assistant for wearing a skirt that was an inch higher than regulation hemlines. Me! The girl who had been voted "most likely to become president" in high school due to her unrelenting moral code, who had testified before the Wisconsin State Legislature on anti-abortion legislation and led prayer groups in her spare time. Now, I was being issued demerits for tardiness to chapel and listening to rock music. It positively fried my compliant, overachieving, firstborn hide.

"I'm a good girl!" I wanted to yell. "I'm on *your side!*" I'd have probably been an RA myself if I hadn't transferred late. Considering my penchant for brownnosery, I'd have probably been awesome at it. Instead, I built up a head of steam and tried to figure out a way to graduate early. I piled on as many credits as possible and fretted about where I would go to graduate school. Because *naturally*, I was going to grad school. College alone would never be enough to prove my value. If I had stayed on at college one more semester, I'd have gotten a second major in linguistics with the addition of just one class. But who needs linguistics? Pshaw. All that study of human language, syntax, grammar. Not writers.

At one point, I was looking at graduate schools in music, journalism, and law, but I was second-guessing all my decisions and scrambling for security in the next steps of my life. I could always be trusted to do the "moral" thing. But now I was looking for someone to tell me what I should do, because I didn't trust myself to do the "correct" thing. What next? What if I totally blew it? The choice of a career became overwhelming. I took the freedom of adulthood and managed to imbue it with the terror of potential defeat.

Someone needed to tell me what to do. Yes, that was it. Someone had to point me in the right direction and give me a little shove. I responded to an unknown prompting and sought out a counselor—a student in a master's program at a local college that was, I'm sure, filling some mandatory service hours so he could graduate. But God uses even lowly student counselors, and simple questions asked on a Monday afternoon, to show us mighty things.

I flopped myself on his ratty sofa. "I don't know what to do after school."

He blinked a set of spectacled eyes at me and asked, "Well, what do you see yourself wearing to work?"

I paused for a second. Because whatever I told him he was going to take as the key to my tomorrow and send me out the door with the promise of a brighter future. I could just feel it, and I had a terrible feeling it was an oversimplification of what to me seemed a very, very big problem.

"Um. A suit?"

"Well, there you go! I think your answer is law school."

I can't remember what I paid him for that session, but I do remember thinking at the time that it had been too much.

I went to the university sports office the next day where I was logging a few hours a week in a work-study program. I thanked my boss for giving me the chance to leave early the previous day so I could go to my "doctor appointment." Was he a doctor? No. An almost-master's level counselor? Yes. But I wasn't in the habit of using the word "counselor" or "therapist" freely. Not for the next thirty seconds, anyway.

"Of course! Are you alright? Is your health good?" she asked sweetly. She was not only the office administrator, she was a den mother to us work-study girls. I loved her then, and now.

I paused for an internal scramble.

"Uh, yes. Well, it's just . . . I am seeing a counselor because I've been . . . sad lately. I just can't figure things out . . ."

"You? Honey, what do *you* have to be depressed about?" She laughed and leaned over the desk to me, reaching for my hand, which she patted with typical kindness. "Well, I'm sure you'll be just fine."

"*Why?*" my mind screamed. "Sarah, you *idiot*! It's no one's business what you do with your time! Now she's going to think you're a nutcase. She'll probably judge you, maybe even tell everyone in the office you're seeing a therapist!" In reality and in retrospect, I'm sure she did neither, but I would not have considered myself to be the model of reasonable thought at that point in my history.

The prospect of judgment is still terrifying to me. For who hasn't judged, themselves? Isn't it a convenient billy club wielded by those of us in the church—that soft, destructive weapon of evisceration that promotes us over another, that assumes we know what God does, and are in a position to say so? In this respect, the Word is clear that we are out of our league (Matt. 7:1), we humans with logs in our eyes, who tsk-tsk those in the church struggling with sin or illness or poor decisions. But don't we all do it? Tell me you haven't seen a bottle of antidepressants on your friend's sink and wondered what goings-on she was subjected to in her head; that you haven't passed a mental hospital and thought, "Thank God I'm not one of those nut jobs." Judgment is so easy, so quiet and convenient.

My first real experience with judgment involving mental health was in my freshman year in college. A good friend of mine, who lived in the same dorm building and with whom I led a Bible study, told me in a moment of vulnerability that she had been diagnosed as bipolar and was on lithium. All I could think was, "Is she going to snap? Am I in danger?" I am wildly ashamed of this. My girlfriend of a year who'd been a confidante of mine, my partner in numerous college escapades, with whom I shared prayers and classes and meals, had revealed a simple diagnosis—nothing more than an ICD-9 code—and I was ready to bolt.

But I know so much better now. I know things, and have experienced things, that make me particularly sensitive to and intolerant of this type of judgment. Let me tell you, from the standpoint of sheer energy expenditure, it's *lots* easier to be transparent and let the chips fall where they may. My friend had done just that. Is it riskier? Absolutely. But you sure don't have to worry about who knows what if everyone knows the same thing. I don't have the stamina to develop a "public" and "private" persona. I'm just too darn exhausted.

When I started law school, I felt myself cower a bit among the other students because of my perceived inadequacy. My classmate in Constitutional Law was a Rhodes Scholar, another was a Fulbright Scholar. Me? I was back to feeling like a hobo. I'd made it in with a strong grade point average, but an average Law School Admissions Test (LSAT) score. "Please, God," I breathed, "let no one ask me what my test scores were, or whether I spent time in the Peace Corps, or whether I founded a charter school for underprivileged children. Also, please let no one ask me if I've spent time working at the mall" (which I had).

After moving to Charlottesville, I began looking for a cat to keep me company. Yes, I thought, a cat would be the *perfect* roommate. A human roommate was out of the question. I had been scarred by freshman year mornings, having crafted the perfect, not-too-early class schedule, only to be awakened by my roommate's hair dryer. Every day. Like she couldn't have let it air-dry for once. I found a beautiful Himalayan with a brown face and blue eyes that I named Portia after Shakespeare's female judge in *The Merchant of Venice*" (a law school student with a cat named after a judge—see what I did there?). She was clean, quiet, and could be managed according to my schedule. Perfect.

My apartment on Cherry Avenue was the first floor of a home rented to me by an elderly lady. She had had the staircase to the second floor drywalled off so as to create enough division for a second apartment upstairs, leaving me a set of stairs to nowhere that I used as a bookcase for my voluminous and growing legal text collection. I hung Victorian art on the walls. My toilet was always clean. I went to class alone, I came home alone. I bought a lot of Lean Cuisines. As I'm writing this, I cannot help but think of that song in *The Music Man*, "Madame Librarian." I was so uptight, I lacked only the topknot hairdo and the skirt with a bustle. Mail arrived for tenants above and below me, but if I'd have tripped over them on the way to my door, I wouldn't have recognized them, so engrossed was I in my tidy, solitary, cat-lady life.

Then, to my great surprise, I was ushered into the world of the U.Va. North Grounds Softball League. *And* I had been selected as one of the commissioners. I did not realize the social import of this at the time. Which is too bad, because I know I missed out on some raging parties. I had received a very late (11 p.m.-ish, which was late for someone who ate dinner at 5:30) phone call from an un-sober classmate who was yelling into the phone that I had to get down to a particular bar that minute because I had been "tapped" as a commissioner.

"What? At this hour?" I croaked. "It's a weeknight!"

Yes, straightlaced was I. Corset-so-tight-I-could-barely-breathe kind of straightlaced. I had my first sip of any alcohol (champagne at a classmate's wedding) at the age of twenty-three. I felt so guilty afterward I cried.

Now, I will probably wake up with a horse head in my bed for saying this, but there is some secret equation for commissioner-hood, though it is never directly spoken of. The proportions are unclear, but it's something like ball playing ability + good looks ÷ potential for partying = commissioner selection rate. I think they got some of the numbers wrong, but I could definitely hit a softball. The problem was, I didn't see myself as someone who fit in. I was terrified at team parties. You'd think I'd been chained in a basement corridor as a child and had stale bread thrown at me like a dog for as good as I was in public. I made a very convincing impression, but my insides quivered like a tuning fork.

So, I stopped going out with my fellow commissioners altogether. Each teammate was given a nickname. Mine (I learned secondhand, because naturally I wasn't present to receive it) was "Carmen San Diego." As in, "Where in the World Is Carmen San Diego?" (of the educational TV show and associated video game). Carmen San Diego is a spy. And the whole point is to find her. Because she's never around. Because she is probably at home with her cat.

On the day of our law school graduation, I learned from one of the girls in my Complex Civil Litigation class that she thought I was a "snob" because of the way I "swept in and out of class alone." I nearly barfed on her shoes explaining that I was really just a big sissy and terribly introverted. I think by the time I was done speaking she had already figured that out for herself.

Now, if you're reading this and have come relatively early to the conclusion that "this girl's a mess," ooh child. Just you wait.

When the time came for the bar exam, I locked myself in the Baltimore apartment into which I'd then moved and spent eight weeks studying. I treated it as my job, because the job I had already accepted with a small litigation firm downtown depended on my passing it. I studied eight to ten hours a day, with a schedule on the refrigerator of what material was to be studied on which days. My eyes spun in my head. Hyper-vigilance, my psyche reminded me. Work harder, never quit, faster, faster, faster! This time, it paid off. I passed the exam on the first try and even scored high enough to wave into the District of Columbia. (Though I'm not actually barred there because at the time I didn't feel like paying the $500 registration fee and it's never actually been a professional impediment, so I add it just to brag, really. It's a brag and an explanation. Yes, a "brag-xplanation.")

School was finally finished. As far as I knew, there were no more exams in my future. There would, however, be many, many tests.

I set up my beanie babies at my desk, hung my diplomas, figured out the billing system, and got down to business.

Beanie babies at a law firm was clue #1 that my choice of profession may have been at least partially misguided.

By the end of the first month, I was already watching the hands on the clock. There was no *Perry Mason*, no *L.A. Law*. It was just a desk and a cityscape and a very expensive degree that went toward boring work I thought I was awful at doing. I could literally hear my creative self committing suicide and I hadn't even made my first school loan payment.

A factor contributory to my misery was my position as the firm's only female lawyer. There were female secretaries and paralegals, but these men had not regularly worked day by day with a woman of equal educational background and brainpower. Clients of mine—two women involved in a real-estate dispute in Baltimore City—told me as the case neared the summary judgment phase and I advised them on next steps that they "had no idea I was a lawyer." They thought I was just another one of the firm's paralegals. Adding insult to injury was the fact that I was asked by one of the partners one morning to get coffee for all the attendees at a deposition. Six figures in student debt, and I had just become a barista.

Now, please don't misunderstand. These men were exceptionally bright and very good at what they did. They loved the Lord and endeavored to represent Him in their profession. If I'd have met them in another capacity, I imagine we'd be fast friends. We just weren't meant to work together. The part of me that was up into the wee hours reading Jack London by a nightlight in high school, the part of me that wrote an extra 2,000 words on my analysis of "Sir Gawain the Green Knight" in college because I was so "into it," was the part of me that needed to leave something that felt mechanical. My professional existence hinged on the billable hour. I churned out legal briefs like a conveyor. The lynchpin was the nature of litigation itself: the us-versus-them mentality that made my stomach hurt. I just wanted everyone to get along. I was certain everything could be worked out without dragging it on in court. I was kicking myself a few months into work, thinking, "Was law school a huge mistake? Oh Lord, help me. So. Much. Debt."

I resolved to leave the firm. It was just a matter of when.

Then, into the firm one day came one of the paralegals who'd just had a baby. She brought with her an infant girl, swaddled in the new fleece of a pink blanket. After one of the partners had held her for a while, squeaking nonsense at the baby in a way none of us, I'm sure, thought him capable of, my paralegal friend turned to me:

"Would you like to hold her?"

"Yes! I'd love to!"

A male partner snorted.

"Well, of course Sarah wants to hold her. She's baby-crazy."

I stared down at a little pink face with prune-like wrinkles, thinking, "Am I emitting some maternal pheromone I'm unaware of?" I hadn't so much as whispered a word to anyone about my plans for children. Socially, I was nothing more than the ex-girlfriend of a number of unsavory ex-boyfriends. I was nowhere near marriage. I had just entered the workforce. I had only a few weeks prior finally figured out the subway system to my office. I fumed quietly. Was I good for nothing more than coffee and babies? What about that big diploma hanging in my office?

It wasn't as if the thought of having children had never occurred to me. Because naturally, I was going to have babies. But I would do so after everything else had fallen into line at the appointed time. And now was certainly not the appointed time. I was going to marry a nice man, establish myself professionally, pay off debt, find a nice home in the suburbs, and then, *only* then, have three children, spaced at appropriate intervals. The sex of these children I would leave up to God. Which was about all I was willing to leave up to Him.

But I was marooned at a job I didn't love, and buried in debt, with nary a suitor in sight. How my plan for children was going to work itself out proved to be yet another anxious puzzle.

Here is where I can look back and see the first intersection of a jumble of decisions that led me someplace meaningful. There is a little silver spider-thread of sense that comes of all this rambling indecision. From my conversation with the student counselor came (a) the initiation of my path to law school. From there, I accepted the job with the law firm (b) in part because they were Christian attorneys. These men discovered *I* was a Christian because (c) my undergraduate alma mater was the college one of the partners had attended, and this was also instrumental in their extending a job offer. After a staff meeting at the firm one morning, (d) one of the partners mentioned a church that might be a good fit for a young professional like me, which (e) is where I went by myself one Sunday morning and heard the youth pastor give an impassioned plea for more volunteers in the high school youth group ministry. And it was a call to which I responded two weeks later, and a ministry in which (f) I met my husband of thirteen years. A man who, as it turned out, also wanted children.

From this protracted jumble of apparent randomness, God pulled something perfectly beautiful. Such a plan He had for me.

He has it still.

~

One Friday afternoon in September of the year 2000, I packed an overnight bag and headed to River Valley Ranch in Manchester, Maryland, for a weekend leaders' retreat as part of the youth ministry at Grace Fellowship Church. Not being one for retreats, I almost bailed. God (as He is wont to do when He has a plan which He desires to execute) made sure I didn't. Someone else needed a ride, and before I knew it, I had a full car and no way to back out. Out to the country I went.

All the leaders in the youth ministry had been brought together as a way to equip them for dealing with teenagers in the coming year. I did not realize how *much* equipping is required for people who deal with teenagers. It's a wonder we weren't there a month. I walked into the lodge for the first evening's session, laughing with a bunch of the other leaders, when a hand appeared above my head and held open the door for us from behind me.

"Y'all better hurry up, or you're gonna be late," said the voice attached to the hand. I turned around.

He was wearing a cowboy hat. A black Stetson. Like an outlaw. If the face below the hat hadn't been so handsome, I might have rolled my eyes at his bluster. Between the drawl and the hat, this dude apparently thought he was Wyatt Earp. But the man's offbeat fashion sense was tempered by good genetics. Plus, he'd opened the door for a group of women, so he appeared to have been raised right. I smiled at him. He smiled back with a mouth full of perfectly white, square teeth. Like Chiclets. I think I saw a tiny sparkle on one of his canines, followed by a, *ding!*

The cowboy bored a hole in my head the whole night. He told me later he was having a conversation with the Lord that went something like, "Lord, I'm here to worship. Let me concentrate on . . . who is that? I wonder if she's single . . . Oops Lord, I'm sorry. Help me listen to what You have to . . . Didn't my roommate say something about a new girl in the group?"

By way of backstory, this man did indeed have a roommate who was in the same ministry, but a different small group. The roommate mentioned to the cowboy one night that there was a girl in his group that the cowboy might be interested in meeting. That she was "curvaceous." I think that was the word. Being gifted with a certain tendency to misread everything, I interpreted this to mean "rotund" or "corpulent." The cowboy would later roll his eyes at this, the first of many eye rolls due to my tendency toward misinterpretation. While I hear both the good stuff and the bad stuff, I only remember the bad stuff. The good stuff I just later go on to misread somehow as bad.

The morning after that first session, I sat at a round table in the cafeteria with ten chairs, nine of which were filled with other women in the ministry. There was one empty chair at the table, and it was next to me. As if it had been planned that way. And because I believe the Lord has a sense of humor, it probably was. Into the chair that morning, with enough bravado for all of us and the next table over, slid the cowboy. He greeted everyone at the table, and then extended his hand to me.

"Hi there. I don't think we've met. I'm Matt Perry." He flashed the Chiclets.

"Hi. I'm Sarah Parshall."

Here's how the rest of it went: Matt Perry followed me around the ranch like a puppy, and before I left to make the drive back to Baltimore, he asked if he could pray for me. We bowed our heads together. But not before he put his arm around my shoulder.

Smooth.

Matt called me two days later to ask me out and showed up four days after that on my front porch with an armful of flowers, wearing a black V-neck sweater and a pair of jeans. He had left the cowboy hat at home. With his good genetics on full display, I almost hit the floor when I opened the door.

That was a Friday. We never stopped going out.

There wasn't a breakup or a "define-the-relationship" conversation. Three weeks after our first date, we sat on my couch together watching football. In the same matter-of-fact way that you might order a sandwich, Matt turned to me and said, "I love you, you know."

"I know," I responded. "I love you too."

As the burnt-earth smell of autumn gave way to early winter, my family prepared for my brother Sam's wedding to his college sweetheart on New Year's Eve. Matt accompanied me, but during what should have been one of the best weekends of my life, I felt as though something was wrong. I felt "off," but couldn't put my finger on it.

After the rehearsal dinner, I dragged myself back to my room and laid shivering in the hotel room bed. I attributed it to overexhaustion, took some ibuprofen, and slept until the next morning. What stands out to me now as I look at pictures of that weekend is how white I was. Mine was the weird, ghostlike face peeking out from the wedding assembly. My glands were the size of limes. After the wedding, I looked at Matt and said, "Please take me back to Baltimore. I think I need to see a doctor."

Matt took me to the hospital the next day. It took a resident one blood test and a physical exam to pronounce, "You have an enlarged spleen. And mononucleosis."

"Wait, what? Mono at twenty-six? That's a teenager's disease!"

The resident replied, "Well, once you're infected, you carry the virus indefinitely. Which means, you caught it from someone who had it in the past." He smirked down at my chart as he scratched some notes. "Probably from kissing."

I looked past the IV bag at Matt, who had only recently gotten over mono himself, and was grinning back at me sheepishly. With what energy I had, I made a little growling sound. At the same time, I also breathed a quiet sigh of relief. Mono meant I could stay home sick from work. When you're thanking God for an enlarged spleen because it means you can call out from work the next day, it's pretty clear you need to get another job.

Five months later, on the Saturday before Mother's Day and on the floor of my parents' Virginia kitchen, Matt knelt down and held open a black velvet box. I burst into tears at the sheer force of happiness that had taken me by surprise. In fact, so surprised was I that I had neglected to wash my hair that day or put on anything nicer than sweatpants because I didn't see it coming. And so, on the day that I would remember for the rest of my life, I was also crying partly because I regretted my unclean hair very, very much. But I guess if a man's willing to take you when you're sporting sweats and a greasy ponytail, there's nowhere to go but up.

My memories of childhood and even of college and school beyond are spotty at best. Certain moments, recounted here, stand out as worthwhile or notable, but it was in that kitchen, on that Saturday, that the memories of my life begin to take shape in a way my previous memories had not. I felt my life coming into focus somehow, the mantles of emotional projection, indecision, and excessive regulation being shrugged off. I sensed my adulthood, finally and at twenty-seven, forming itself onto a skeleton of co-partnership and co-reliance with someone who loved me as desperately as I did him. Though my cat-lady independence waned, I felt oddly alive.

I was embarking, however, with someone I barely knew into a future we had no idea would wear us down to our exposed nerves.

We were married seven months later—a memorably awful affair. The bulk of conventional wisdom would have told us to avoid a wedding on the biggest travel weekend of the year: Thanksgiving. It would have also told us to avoid picking a reception site forty-five minutes from the wedding site, heading north into Washington, DC (because there is no traffic, ever, on the DC beltway—*especially* not on a holiday weekend). It was a rainy, disorganized, emotionally charged event in an overheated inn where the well-paid DJ played for no one but a few of the kids who hadn't passed out from heatstroke, and some of the most important people in my life snuck out the back door before the cake was even cut. In retrospect, I can hardly blame them. I think we were there long enough for the earth to make one full rotation around the sun.

When it was finally over, Matt and I dragged our soggy, married selves back down the interstate in the direction we had come, to the Kenmore Inn in Fredericksburg, Virginia, for our first night as a married couple. As Matt and some of the groomsmen transferred wedding gifts between cars, I stood in front of the teenage desk clerk in a giant ball gown with a mud-blacked hem, my hair deflated by the misting rain and my makeup beginning to migrate south. The clerk shuffled some papers and scanned a computer screen with increasing apologetic intensity. It was then that I learned she'd been substituting for someone else. Also, that she'd been unable to find our reservation and had given the honeymoon suite away to someone else. We were relegated to the smallest of the double-occupant rooms and slept in a full-size bed (barely enough room for Matt's 6'1", 250+ pound frame, let alone both of us), next to a bathroom reminiscent of a high school locker room with yellow floor-to-ceiling tile and industrial faucets spouting from the most unlikely of places. I was waiting for Ashton Kutcher to jump out and tell me I'd been "punk'd."

To this day, I do not look back on my wedding day with the sentimentality of most wives. I get sour, instead. And then I force Matt into yet another discussion about what we *should* have done, and alternatively, what we *will* do when our twenty-fifth anniversary rolls around (hint: Fiji).

But our wedding was just one day. Just one day in a lifetime that was getting ready to really test our mettle.

~

It all started with a trash can. A dented, rusted trash can with the Dallas Cowboys logo. It looked like something you'd find a bunch of homeless people using for a bonfire under a bridge in the middle of winter. The minute it moved into our condo, I smiled daintily at Matt and plotted in silence about how to remove it. He wanted it in our office. I wanted it gone. It was puncturing the walls with its pointy edges, and he wouldn't get rid of it. The rust came off in bits on my hand when I emptied it, and he still wouldn't get rid of it.

This was the first real exercise of dominion and control Matt and I had undertaken in our brief marriage. When you're madly in love and engaged after six months, you lack the opportunity to ask if one of you is a control freak. Or, for that matter, whether one of you has anger issues and happens to ignite quicker than a Roman candle in July. Which Matt did.

Three months in, Matt and I were hollering at each other. Rather, Matt was hollering, and I was cowering, as this is my modus operandi in fights. I cower and drop my eyes and cease talking altogether in the hopes that the other person will just get tired of their own tirade and move on after a while. This usually works. For Matt, all it did was provoke him. He wanted me to concede, he wanted to battle. He was fighting to be right, not for reconciliation, but fighting was still a method of engagement. Matt is energized by relationships and driven by the need to connect with other people. This is why he is so good at his job in sales. But when you're fighting with someone (which, he might have argued, was the ultimate manner of engagement) and they totally shut down, all this does is succeed in further infuriating you. During one early point in our marriage, Matt flung his wedding ring across the room so hard he pitted the drywall. He had packed a bag and was headed for the door.

"I didn't sign on for this!" he yelled. About something stupid. Because whatever it was, I can't remember it now and neither can he.

"Fine," I responded with forced coolness. "I don't care." But I did care. I cared very much, and I was scared he was not coming back.

This was but the first in a number of spitting-mad scenarios wherein one of us would make as though we were leaving, and the other would subsequently blow up that person's phone in an attempt to hunt them down and apologize. A word to you married folk out there: gaining a little space is fine, but don't make as though you're never coming back. It's just plain mean. And really, it's not convincing anyone if you leave with nothing more than an overnight bag. At some point, you have to come back for the rest of your stuff.

~

My parents' generation married early. Think nineteen-years-old early. A girlfriend of mine just married at thirty-nine. This is our generation. Matt and I were well established in our careers, our patterns, our peccadilloes before we met. Ironically, what we thought was our readiness for marriage turned out likewise to be stubbornness in ways of thinking and behaving. The longer you live on your own, the less easily you relinquish control of your life to someone else.

I shoved Matt into the appreciation of a clean house, ways of decorating, things we ate. Matt shoved me into commitments with more people than I could count, which for an introvert is exhausting and requires at least two days' recuperation. I used to "joke" (and I use quotations here because I've always been of a mind that it's easier to pass off saying the hard stuff with a nervous giggle) that I married Matt and all his friends because our home was never empty. Matt also forced me into a more relative interpretation of the phrase "on time," because the last thing he was really on time for was our wedding. Everything since then has been a downhill slide into tardiness.

Wanna guess what this does for someone who's naturally anxious?

Then there were certain of my psychological misconceptions—those I held before I was married and upon which I had never been called to account. Chief among them were these: I'm not frenzied, just intense; not anxious, just insistent. After I was married, when Matt noticed I was white-knuckling everything from puppy obedience classes to the cleanliness of the bathroom grout, he tactfully suggested:

"Honey, I think you have a problem."

"Why do you always think the problem is with me?" I would snort. "What if you just can't manage things like I can? Maybe the problem is with you!"

"This problem *is* about you," he would retort. "Do you know how hard it is to try to manage every environment so that your wife doesn't head into some anxious or depressive tailspin? Why are you trying so hard? It's exhausting both of us! What would happen if you didn't?"

"Didn't *what*?"

"Try so hard!"

This stumped me. The only thing I could manage was, "Well . . . then everything would fall apart!"

But I didn't know what that meant, or whether it was true, or for whom it would fall apart. I just knew that the fear of it happening was enough to keep me gripping and pushing and striving. It was enough to sacrifice the both of us on the psychological altar of my own making.

I could hear the Lord in my ear after these conversations. There was a swirling sensation in my gut, one that spoke of a way of life that was being interrupted. He was stirring things up and using my husband to fan a little spark of unhappiness into a flame by questioning the reasons behind my way of being. But changing my entire way of thinking was as unsettling to me as it was to consider the prospect of having things fall apart.

"This isn't about you or him," the Lord whispered into my heart. "It's about both of you. And it's about Me. It will always, in some measure, be about Me."

I was sitting at the kitchen island in our little yellow farmhouse now. We'd moved from the Baltimore condominium we had shared after getting married, and had taken our anxiety and rage with us into our new home. Something had to change. Particularly because the pair of us were about to become a trio.

I picked Portia up, setting her down in my lap and pulling one of her fine white hairs off my lip. She resisted my advances and jumped off. Pretty, she was, but the nastiest cat I ever knew. The only person she could stand was Matt.

Naturally.

I felt the Lord prodding: "I require the sacrifices of both of you for the good of the whole of you."

I didn't want to listen to the Lord, but He insisted on talking. He's like that, you know. Always getting His point across one way or another.

"What sacrifices? I've pretty much given everything up."

"Please! You lack for nothing. Your neck is stiff, and you know full well what I've said about being anxious [Phil. 4:6]. How you think and behave is changing your marriage for the worse. If you will only obey Me and let Me help you, then you and Matt will thrive. But if you keep turning away and refusing to listen to the reasons behind the discontent I'm allowing to fester within you, then you will fail [Isa. 1:19–20]. Your behavior is no longer exhausting the resources of your own life, it's exhausting those of your family. It is time to get help."

Getting help started with admitting—at Matt's suggestion—that maybe Portia had to go. Perhaps sensing the impending arrival of a small person, our cat started peeing on our guest room bed, which set off a daily bedding change and a small freak-out on my part. She also started batting her paws and kicking out at anything that came near. She hissed at visitors and hid under the bed. I had owned Portia from the age of six weeks and she was acting like she'd been waterboarded. She went from antisocial to downright intolerable. We found a young college girl to take her. The pedigreed kitty from the uptight future mother went on to a far more relaxed lifestyle. I imagine her to this day splayed out on some sun-splashed floor in a condo in the middle of a busy metropolis where she isn't offended by children or other pets and can follow the new money back and forth from the Whole Foods store across the street. She's probably thinking she's gotten the lifestyle to which she's always aspired.

Getting help also meant that (kicking and screaming the whole way to the office for our first session) I began counseling with a Christian therapist. This was my only condition: that my counselor be a Christ follower. For how does a person separate her mind from her soul? But I wasn't about to tell anyone—even the man the Lord had designed to know me most intimately—that I thought there was even a whiff of a problem. You see, my philosophy of robotic life perfection resulted in planning, that resulted in a predictability, that resulted in some kind of tiny, temporary peace. It lasted for, like, five minutes. But I liked that peace. I didn't want to go chucking the system. Who knew what would happen?

The first few months, I did nothing but cross my arms and stare at my therapist. When I did talk, it was a volcano of words about nothing. This weather is crazy, right? Where should we go on vacation? What do you think about Matt's job offer? To quote a writer far better than me, it was all sound and fury, signifying nothing. She suggested Prozac. I suggested she shove it. Medicine was for crazy people.

Crazy cat ladies with crazy minds who can't let go.

Eh, I thought. Maybe I'll give it a shot.

3

There Must Be Some Mistake

Before I formed you in the womb I knew you,
and before you were born I consecrated you.

Jeremiah 1:5 ESV

Control and I were in a battle to the death.

OK, "battle" is a bit of a misnomer, because "battle" indicates opponents of equal force and capability. Control was stronger than me, and it was winning.

But I wasn't the only one who was losing. My husband was losing. My friends were losing. My relationship with the Lord? Who has time for that when you're squeezing the life out of life? The desire to perfectly manipulate every situation was giving me an ulcer, and while I didn't know it, I was also speeding the clock hands of my life. It's a wonder my face doesn't look like an old shoe. I was losing time with the people who mattered and losing the opportunity to do what was fulfilling and important. Instead, I was cracking down on making perfect Asian dumplings. I can barely type that sentence without laughing. I remember cutting the powdered dough and pinching its corners around a little sphere of pork before dropping it into the boiling broth prior to Matt's arrival one evening. Ginger salad, sticky rice, lit candles—these were the trappings that went with. What a treat I must have been for the "old" Matt. We couldn't stop fighting, but I'll tell you what, the man ate like a king. If I had that kind of extra time now, I would just take a nap.

My life's imbalance was obvious to most everyone except me. Which is why I'm fairly certain the Good Lord in His infinite wisdom gave me children who are atypical in a great many ways. The first of these atypical children is my oldest. Should I speculate on God's timing here, I would say He wanted to get the message through as quickly as possible, before I went on to have two more children who lent a hand in discombobulating all of us.

God was about to show me how terribly messy a parent's life is, from the catastrophes we never saw coming to the weird things I find in my children's beds. Because here's the thing about parenting: if you have control issues before you have kids, there's a pretty good chance you're going to have a legitimate come-to-Jesus moment after they're born. I was about to hit a brick wall and couldn't do a thing about it. For a control freak, this is the ultimate waking nightmare. It's also where the next part of my story begins.

Our discussion about when to try getting pregnant was pretty much like all the other decisions we've made in our lives. There was very little buildup, and within about ten minutes, we were wholly committed. "Head first, deep end," as Matt says. Don't take investment advice from us, by the way.

Over dinner one night, I asked Matt, "Well, when do you think we should start trying to get pregnant? I mean, we've been married for two years . . ."

"Now seems like a good enough time."

"OK."

Just like that . . . done.

We are many things; indecisive, we are not. Prior to our union, I was queen waffler and might have been content to keep it that way. More room for anxiety and whatnot. But as it turns out, Matt can be just as persuasive as I am and possibly more so when faced with a case to make, though he relies far more than I do on the emotional plea and casting of a grand vision. In this vein, and after we married, I was swept up in my husband's "if not now, when?" rationale. He was like a supernova—so full of largesse and hilarity and geniality. I had never seen the likes of him. He sucked me into the romance of the spur-of-the-moment commitment with all its immediate possibility for fulfillment. In retrospect, I suppose the rather hasty decision he made to marry me could have been a disaster if the Lord hadn't directed the whole thing from the start. Thank God *that* quick decision turned out to be right. Now, the blistering pace at which we move on resolutions is legend among our friends. A pastor friend of ours said once that we "live life big": the kind of people who get an idea and roll. We would be perfect marks for a Ponzi scheme. Once we get past the initial concept, we're all in. I can tell you it's virtually impossible to maintain financial integrity with this kind of commitment to perpetual movement. It's saddled us with everything from animals to houses to appliances. These things came to us in the era of easy living. Before we knew what it was to make decisions with consequences that would cut us to the core.

This is why, when we decided to get pregnant, we also thought we needed a vacation to accomplish it. To the island of St. Kitts. Not Atlantic City, not the Outer Banks of North Carolina. No, we required a trip to an exotic Leeward Island where a five-star Marriott was offering low introductory rates for Marriott rewards members. Because the deal "sounded good." Two tickets to a babymoon later, we were stepping off the commuter jet and onto a tarmac ringed by volcanic mountains in a part of the Caribbean then little-known to tourists. The airport was about the length of a football field from one end to the other, domed by a hot, blue sky punctuated with occasional clouds. Giant palms stretched their leaves upward.

Weren't we just the luckiest people on earth?

I hate to tip Marriott off here, but the $99 a night we paid for the room was a steal. The resort had four pools, five restaurants, catamaran cruises, a private beach, and a casino (you know, if you're *into* that kind of thing). We congratulated ourselves on the discovery of this paradise. We toured the island in the tiniest jeep you've ever seen. I think it was only slightly larger than the current model Barbie car. We hopped off at every stop, visiting abandoned sugar plantations and an artist's studio set high above the bay. We discovered an overgrown path leading to what will be forever known as "sneaky beach": a strip of white sand bordered by skyward hills and a forgotten, weather-worn concession stand from which coconuts or jerk chicken were probably once sold. There grazed a raft of goats belonging to no one in particular. We felt like someone had shuttled us back to the Garden of Eden.

I'm sure it comes as no surprise that we left the island pregnant. Thank you, St. Kitts and Nevis Department of Tourism.

When I took a pregnancy test a few weeks later, I almost fell over. I thought it was broken. So I took four more. The ground beneath my feet surged upward and I started sweating. Uh, what? It worked already? Wait . . . is there another person inside me?

In typical fashion, one of the tests I had bought used words instead of the usual double lines to indicate pregnancy. Because lines can be faint or strong. Lines can be ambiguous. A word is different. A word indicates "yes" or "no" with no hint of ambiguity. A word provides control and direction. This test screamed "*pregnant.*" I showed the test to Matt. He said later that when he saw it, the word "pregnant" jumped out at him like it was in 3-D. It separated from the test like the eyes of a cartoon wolf do when the wolf sees a female wolf: "*ar-oo-gah!*" Matt said he had the following thought: "How can this be? I'm only *eighteen*!"

In reality, he was nearing thirty-one. He was, statistically, closer to having a child with a neurological disability than he had been at any previous point in his life.

We both were.[1]

The next summer, the seventeen-year cicadas pushed through the ancient roots of our pear tree and swarmed the house with their helicopter droning. They were so thick in the trees that if we used a phone anywhere near our front yard, we couldn't be heard on the other end. I had to flick them off the crib one by one as it was delivered to the house. Pregnant as a zephyr with this first child, perpetually sweaty in the July heat, I had the impression something momentous was about to happen. It felt very much like the scene in one of those end-of-times movies where the sky grows dark with the coming onslaught of locusts. Or cicadas. Cicadas so thick you have to pick them out of your hair while screaming to your husband in a hormonal rage that you can't take it anymore.

I felt the joy of our upcoming introduction—this boy and me—but I knew the perfect cube of my life was slowly and ungraciously expanding its borders. Which is why I was prone to such prenatal psychosis as calling my best friend and pleading with her to come (waddle) with me to Home Depot because I absolutely had to have a patio umbrella for the deck because we didn't have an awning, and *how was I supposed to sit outside with my newborn baby if the sun was going to cook him like a chicken?* My mind was telling me: "It's all gonna be perfect as long as you keep everything perfectly managed." Everyone else was telling me, "Girl, you have lost your ever-loving mind." In retrospect, I might have been the tiniest bit like Lennie Small in *Of Mice and Men*. If I'd had a puppy that summer, I might have petted it to death. I only had so much time left before this person came out of me to get everything just right, because I was pretty sure I couldn't control a baby and he was going to mess a few things up. I had seemed to remember reading somewhere that kids were messy.

I figured I'd just get to that later.

I felt changes further afoot when I handed a three-page, single-spaced birth plan adorned with ridiculous cartoon storks to the nurses at the hospital and they burst out laughing. I scowled at them, as they had clearly misunderstood the level of perfection I was going to dedicate to motherhood as I had everything else in my life. I thought about opening my mouth to counter their snickering, but a swelling contraction and a deep-rooted sense of saving face kept my mouth shut. I am a descendant of a long line of deferential people and there's nothing I hate more than being embarrassed. The Lord would eventually provide lots of opportunities here. Like a full-on raging meltdown in a grocery store on a Saturday afternoon, before a football game, when the line for checkout snakes all the way back to produce.

On that sweltering July day when our first child made his entrance, I had everything from my "focus picture" (you know, the one the birthing coaches tell you to focus on when you're pushing so you won't mistakenly send out a kidney instead of a human) to my bag of scented toiletries at the ready. I had even gone so far as to pack a tidy little bag of snacks and beverages for my husband so that he wouldn't be tempted to walk down two flights to the cafeteria and leave me in the hands of the smirking nurses who were liable to turn off the epidural or something, since they thought my birthing plan was such a farce. From this bag, and at some point during hour three (yes, t-h-r-e-e, though it would finally be over f-o-u-r) of pushing, my husband pulled his chocolate chip granola bar from the bag. As Matt leaned down into my shoulder to talk me through yet another contraction, a cloud of granola spewed forth.

I turned to him and screamed, "You smell like chocolate!"

I had managed everything leading up to the birth, but not my stunning, unprovoked rage at the smell of granola. Granola I had so tenderly packed for him.

Matt did, in fact, make it down to the cafeteria.

Thirty-six hours doesn't seem like much when the clock is moving at a normal rate. But when it's slowed to a crawl because of the vice-like grip another person has on your insides, you will pretty much grab the first passerby to help pull that person out. Complicating things was the fact that our son's weight was woefully underestimated. A glib nurse in triage had pushed a bit on my belly and proclaimed, "Probably seven and a half." She may as well have said "seven and a half *grams*" for as accurate as she was not. My fifty-two-pound weight gain had done a bang-up job of camouflaging his size, and our baby had become stuck in the birth canal. After an internal fetal scalp monitor for his dipping heart rate, discussions of an emergency C-section, something about a forceps that my mind has subsequently erased, and a male resident laying across my midsection to squeeze him out, Noah Paul Perry arrived at nine pounds, slightly blue, quite jaundiced, but fully, mercifully intact.

There was no crying, no "ta-da!" at his entrance. My son was silent. It was many minutes before I saw him again.

When I did, when Noah was finally delivered to us as the most wonderful gift ever, I remember that his head was pyramidal from being stuck in the birth canal for so long. His skin was yellow from jaundice, and he sported a great shock of black hair that neither Matt nor I could account for. I looked up at my husband.

"Um, is it just me, or is he kinda ugly?"

Matt laughed. "Yes, he is."

Visitors to our room oohed and aahed over him, and we offered them all the same caveat:

"It's OK. You don't have to say he's cute. We know he's sort of goofy looking."

I'm still the object of criticism about this by some of my friends.

Does this make us the worst parents ever? I don't know. I don't think the perception of a child's beauty in any way diminishes a parent's love for that child. I know it didn't in our case, because when they laid the heavy bundle of our son on my chest, I felt a kind of blessed euphoria that gave new meaning to the verse from Psalm 127:3 that says children are a reward from the Lord. I was wiping from Noah's small face my tears of elation and gratitude. "I love you," I whispered to him. "Thank You," I whispered to God.

We positively adored him.

~

I don't know exactly when the perception of Noah's disability rose up to me like smoke from a pyre. It is said that mothers are possessed of a sixth sense, a preternatural ability to determine when their children are in danger. If I were anyone else, I might write my awareness off to this convenient little maxim, but in truth, God was nudging me with a quiet, determined hand.

I remember first uttering the words "I think Noah might be autistic" when he was eighteen months old. His late walking, late talking, repetitive hand flapping, and his difficulty looking me in the face all gave it away. His tantrums were earth shattering. His sensory difficulties were stymieing. We begged off on birthday parties or took him to another room because the strains of "Happy Birthday to You" set him to fits of screaming. I now realize he hates things that are loud.

In typical first-time-mother style, I pored over the packet they sent us home with from the hospital. Because this is what you do for your first child. You are convinced you aren't going to even remember to change this little human's diaper unless you follow a precise diagram and a routine schedule. Like the smell or the density of that thing under the onesie is not going to give it away.

In the instructional packet, I found a coupon to have a photo representative come to the house and perform a photo session of my baby boy when he was ten months old. One of the photos from this session I carry with me to this day: it is a picture of Noah, his hands in mid-flap, his body stiffened, and his mouth agape, just so excited that he cannot express it any other way.

I knew then what no one else knew.

But he was affable, sociable, and an easy laugher. He liked people. And more than that, he utterly lacked stranger anxiety (which, though charming at the time, has since been revealed to us as a potential indicator for autism). Not surprisingly, I was called alarmist. A lot.

"You've got to be kidding me," a teacher friend insisted.

"There's no way," his primary care pediatrician countered. "He's eccentric. That hand flapping is just his excited reaction to things he likes."

Yes. And maybe something else, I thought.

Even Matt had a hard time buying the theory. "Honey, he's fine. You worry too much."

Yes, I thought again. And maybe it's something else.

Though I knew little of "normal" developmental behavior—Noah was our first, and we were the first among our friends to have children—something, Someone, told me to persist. God's hand prompted me forward, and I pushed on, determined. "Let's just make sure there's nothing wrong with him so we can get on with our lives," I told Matt. My heart felt something coming; my mind had not yet acquiesced. As Matt, Noah, and I walked into the Kennedy Krieger Institute's Center for Autism and Related Disorders in Baltimore, I quickly prayed that I had been wrong, that maybe I had been over-reactionary after all.

Our neurologist solved that problem in about five minutes.

"He's definitely on the autism spectrum, likely Asperger's, but at five, it's hard to pin that down. We'll need more time. He also has ADHD, oppositional defiance disorder, and obsessive compulsive disorder. You were lucky to get a diagnosis so early. We can start intervention now."

This is the part in the movie where two guys are about to get in a brawl, and while one of them is looking down to roll up his sleeve, the other one clocks him with a right hook.

The rest of the meeting went approximately like this:

"Blah blah blah, blah blah blah." Oh, and this: "High functioning is a bit of a misnomer. This will be with him all his life, and he's going to have to work very hard to assimilate."

That's pretty much all we heard after the first part.

What is it like when you hear words like this from a world expert on autism? How do you feel when your five-year-old boy is playing with the slats on the blinds in the doctor's office instead of interacting with the people around him or investigating the abundant toys on the shelf? How does it feel when someone way above your pay grade has told you that this is something you're going to have to make peace with because it's not going to change? It feels like there must have been a mix-up in administration, and perhaps a responsibility of this magnitude was supposed to have gone to someone better prepared to handle it. You were just prepared for a regular ol' garden-variety toddler. You're pretty sure there's been some kind of mistake.

Later on in my mother's journey, I attended a disabilities conference and came across a poem[2] that perfectly summarized the way it felt when what I suspected about my son was verified by someone who was expert at doing so. It feels like you've planned for a trip to one specific country, and because the pilot has altered the plane's course mid-flight, you instead step foot on the tarmac in a country for which you are wholly unprepared; like packing for Italy and learning to speak Italian and dreaming of cannoli at the foot of the Piazza Di Spagna, and instead, finding yourself in Holland, in the land of windmills and wooden shoes and waving tulips. Of course I have come in time to appreciate that place for its own unique beauty and unexpected treasures. I have, over time, learned to speak Dutch. But sometimes in the hushed moments, I still wonder what Italy might have been like.

After we left the clinic, we stumbled to a local restaurant to have lunch with a hungry little boy and nurse our wounds. Matt cried. He called family and friends. He fumbled around for support. Me? I was quiet as a slab of stone. Because I could only think one thing:

We were on foreign soil.

As he grew, Noah demonstrated odd tendencies that we didn't fully understand as being connected to his autism. Take food, for example. Noah has sensory difficulties that make mealtimes a bit challenging because certain textures and smells cause him to vomit. He can quite nearly do it on cue. A plate of his strawberries fell to the floor yesterday near a strand of dog hair, and in an instant, his eyes welled up and the retching started.

I still remember the day Noah screamed about sand in his peanut butter and jelly sandwich. *Sand.* The closest beach is nearly two hours from here. I can testify that there was nothing in his sandwich, but it didn't prevent him from demonstrating his strong contrary belief all over the kitchen floor. For Noah, there was something tiny and out of order in his meal, something that changed its entire composition. To this day, I cannot change the sensations that Noah dislikes, the foods he refuses to eat. There are a lot of things I cannot change about my life or his. Wanting to change things, worrying about achieving things once perceived as perfect and desirable does not change anything. God is teaching me both mind and finger control. As in, I have to make up my mind to peel my sweaty fingers off the wheel.

A few years later, the sequels to "Noah" were released. Two and a half years after Noah, came "Grace." Two and a half years after Grace, came "Jesse." I would like to say the symmetry of timing here was my doing, but alas, I cannot claim credit. Which is too bad. It would have been one of the few facets of my "life plan" to unfold with perfect accuracy.

Last year, we enrolled all three in a small Christian school that had loved Noah so well before the other two arrived. The three of them would be each other's support, their backups. There was peace on the home front.

Grace was off to kindergarten with braided hair, buckle shoes, and the cooing of her teachers. She is not only dimpled and precocious, but she is lightning quick. Early walker, early talker, early for school. (Seriously. I wouldn't make it out the door on time if she didn't scream at all of us that we were going to be late if we didn't leave *right this minute!*)

It was also three-year-old Jesse's first time in a school program of any sort. For over a year, I'd taken Jesse to music classes and story times, playgrounds and sporting events; anything to get him appropriately socialized in preparation for the upcoming school year. He was excited to follow in Noah and Grace's footsteps. He wasn't the only one. "Freedom!" I hollered to Matt. I deposited them in their classrooms on the first day of school and had to stifle a fist pump I was so psyched. Fantasies of mornings on the porch with my laptop and a cup of coffee abounded. Perhaps I am of a different breed than those crying-on-the-first-day mothers. I am, I think, more of the crying-when-the-school-year-ends type. I mean, I'm going to get them back in only seven hours. That is not nearly enough time to miss them. I was also foolhardy enough to think that with the kids out of the house, I was going to get our lives finally under control. I would have everything organized, everything managed, everything up-to-date.

What a delusional fool I was.

Within the first four days of school, Jesse came home with a disciplinary note. "Hitting," "kicking," and "destroying," his teachers wrote. At home, there was "frowning," "hair pulling," and "sighing."

When Jesse was eighteen months old, we took him to be evaluated by the Kennedy Krieger Institute—the same highly respected clinic from which Noah's diagnoses sprung. Our pediatric neurologist had suggested that we have all our kids evaluated for developmental delays because these things do run in families, with a particular predilection for brothers. Statistics show that the risk of an autism spectrum disorder (ASD) diagnosis for male infants who have an older sibling with ASD is greater than 26 percent.[3]

During his initial evaluation, Jesse was diagnosed with a language delay. But without therapy or intervention, the delay righted itself in three months. He went from a five-to-ten-word vocabulary to complete sentences in the time it takes for Katy Perry to dye her hair. We skated by for a while, and marveled at the detailed conversations we were able to have with our toddler. Think, "Of course I'm not going to school, Mom, that's ridiculous!" kind of verbal. Or, "That firefighter will certainly fall off that ladder because it's far too tall for him" sort of verbal. These were things he said at two and three years old. Hey, everyone! Look at this super-smart kid of ours!

Jesse was energetic, funny, and musically gifted. But he was also clumsy, obsessed with fire trucks, prone to the singular arrangements of objects, and preferred to play by himself. His memory was just as exceptional as his brother's. I began to add things up after Jesse's immediate aggression toward other kids in the first week of school, and the way he spit at people in Walmart.

Dang it. Really? Another one?

A year after we had Jesse's initial evaluation, Jesse started spinning, his fixations increased, and the self-injurious behavior started. After a few follow-ups at Kennedy Krieger, we got what we already knew was coming: a little group of diagnoses that include PDD-NOS (an autism "sub-type" that is now, just as Asperger's is, simply called "autism spectrum disorder," according to the most recent edition of the *Diagnostic and Statistical Manual of Mental Disorders*), along with ADHD and OCD. Like his brother. Somewhere in the mix may be another diagnosis, but our neurologist is waiting to see what develops as Jesse matures.

Fantastic, I thought. Two brothers, seven disabilities of distinction. This is gonna cost us a fortune.

After Jesse's neurological report was handed to us, I started to think that somewhere in our genetic code something went off the rails. None of us can pinpoint its timing, but there is some speculation that our family's former hometown in Wisconsin had something to do with it. For over a century, the city's well water has contained radium, a naturally occurring radioactive material that contributes to an increased risk of cancer when ingested in high doses or over an extended period of time. As I approached my high school reunion, I was deluged with stories about classmates with cancer, multiple sclerosis, rare autoimmune diseases, and more. In my own family, we've had four cases of blood-borne cancer within two generations, my own autoimmune disease (fun fact! more on that later), my boys' autism, and my niece's apraxia. Friends of mine from the same high school also have children with substantial developmental disabilities. One former classmate not only has lupus herself, she also has a child with ASD and another with Rett syndrome (an extremely rare pervasive developmental disorder that almost exclusively affects girls).

Autism spectrum disorder has a strong genetic basis, but its connection is complex, and some have speculated that ASD is explained more by multigene interactions or by rare mutations (i.e., something in the environment that tinkered with the genetic code, occurring in the DNA of individual cells, and known as acquired or somatic mutations) than by a single inherited gene.[4] Like maybe, oh, I don't know, long-term exposure to radioactive water? I'm not a scientist, but I'd wager that the water we were all drinking would have been better in the toilet than the tap.[5] Call it a hunch.

It does make a girl wonder what, if they should have children, my own kids might bequeath to future generations. I remember well a conversation Matt and I had before our first pregnancy. Before the carefree trip to St. Kitts and a fistful of pregnancy tests paved the way for the kind of dreams parents have for their neurotypical[6] children—those not on the autism spectrum.

It went something like this:

Sarah: "Matt, I'm worried."

Matt: "Oh, OK. Great. Because *that's* something new." (*"That" is in italics because my Dell doesn't have a sarcasm key.*)

Sarah (*rolling eyes*): "C'mon. We have a lot of nasty stuff between our two families. What if we pass something down?"

Matt: "We probably will."

Sarah: "So what—are we just going to avoid having kids?"

Matt: "Is that what you want?"

Sarah: "No. You know I want kids."

Matt: "OK, well, so do I. So if we have them, I guess the Lord wants them for us, which means He also wants them to have whatever they come with. That part is totally beyond our control. Out of control means there's nothing to do but trust Him. He'll take care of them, regardless."

Sarah: "Even if they have your big head? I mean, that's really an enormous skull you've got there."

Matt: "Oh they definitely will. This thing?" (*tapping on his heavy-boned forehead*) "It holds all the brains."

We have since developed a theory that the three easiest life choices involve real estate, jobs, and children because you either get them or you don't, making God's answer for each a pretty clear "yes" or a "no." It turns out God's answer for us concerning children was a "yes." It was an electrifying, ear-splitting "yes," that sounded to Matt like the cartoon wolf's *"ar-oo-gah!"* It was also a "yes" to the things that make them different, and a "yes" to the Lord always providing for them.

As it so happened, it was also a "yes" to their big heads. Each one of their noggins is in the 75 percent or higher range.

At the time, though, we weren't thinking about the psychological impact these diagnoses would have on us as parents, and on me, mother micromanager in particular. Now I had something else to be anxious about. Consistent with my theories of hypervigilance altering the course of the universe, I was convinced that I had an opportunity for colossal failure or major success. Doing my best and leaving the rest to the Lord was not a thing for me.

There was the "How do we pay for this?" and "Will they ever be able to hold down a job?" inquiries. There was "Where do they go for physical therapy?" followed by "How can I minimize the tics and fixations because I don't want them ridiculed?" And there were major concerns about their education. Do we mainstream them or enroll them in special education classes? Is the small Christian school that loves them but has no individual educational process (I.E.P.) experience better than the large public school that has experience dealing with developmental disabilities and can help us develop an I.E.P., but who might treat them as just another face in the crowd?

I spent a lot of time lying in bed and staring at the ceiling, wondering how I was going to wrestle my circumstances back into obedience.

"Nice try," I could hear the Lord saying. "You just keep on squeezing that steering wheel and see how much good it does you."

"But, Lord!" I silently cried (though I could have screamed it, because my sleeping husband has bragged about being able to fall asleep in the bleachers at a football game and I'm certain he would have kept right on snoring), "I don't know how to do things 'right' with this autism stuff. This is new territory. I'm just marginally freaking, you know."

"I know." I could feel Him next to me, smiling at my hamster-on-a-wheel hysteria. "Listen, I don't abandon the work of My hands [Ps. 138:8]. I created your boys. Do you think any part of them is a mistake? My power is made perfect in all their earthly weaknesses, in all the places they will struggle [2 Cor. 12:9]. I made them perfectly, for this time and purpose. So that My power might be shown through them [Exod. 9:16].

"And I made them for you, Sarah. You needed them. You needed their uniqueness to overcome your own challenges."

"Yeah," I sighed, shifting my body and settling into another restless night. "I thought You might say that."

~

We have since learned that who our boys truly are doesn't change because of a medical label. Their behavior isn't easier to manage just because someone in an office in Baltimore has given what they have a name. Of course, it changes how they are educated. It changes how we spend our free time as we look for appropriate therapies. It alters the tactics we employ during their most difficult struggles. Heaven knows it changes the food I buy (there's only so much puke I can manage in a week). But a diagnostic code on a discharge slip means more to our insurance company than it does to us. That's right, Aetna. We're coming for you.

With three children and a host of diagnoses, my husband and I were thrown headlong into a lifestyle we could not have anticipated, one full of challenges unknown to the parents of neurotypical children: disbelieving critics, expensive thera-pies, social struggles. But there were also the challenges that come with every "typical" child: the ones who try to ride the dog, or finger-paint with mustard, or unflinchingly ask you, "Mom, if you'd just do my homework for me, it would be a real help. Thanks." Mine is the story of every parent's life, because every kid is expensive and requires special treatment, and every kid—whether you want to admit it or not—can push you to the point of locking yourself in the bathroom so you can surf the internet and finally get around to clipping your toenails.

Every kid requires the kind of blind faith that comes with turning the whole parenting thing over to God. Even when—*especially when*—you land in Holland.

4

Sibling Misery

Behold, children are a heritage from the LORD,
  the fruit of the womb a reward.
Like arrows in the hand of a warrior
  are the children of one's youth.
Blessed is the man
  who fills his quiver with them!

Psalm 127:3–5 ESV

A Chinese proverb on children says "One is like none, and two are like ten." I imagine this proverb is rooted somewhere in the notion that if a parent has only one child, that child—like an animal born in the wild—has no natural enemies and is not capable of fighting himself for the television remote. For us, the work of multiple children centers mostly on trying to prevent a triple homicide.

I once fawned and tittered over our single child, Noah. I sanitized like a surgeon, I crammed full his baby book.

73

I even ironed his many, many clothes. I have since learned that unless a child is older than, say, twelve, or headed to a professional photo shoot, such care toward the appearance of clothes is only warranted if you have an abundance of free time or think you might be able to consign them later for cash. Children are veritable Rembrandts when it comes to making kempt things unkempt.

Matt and I thought we had the single-child thing nailed so well that we took Noah on not one but two international trips. I have photos of a beaming Noah in a carrier on Matt's back on the island of St. John and, later, holding my hand as we strolled the Irish National Stud in County Kildare, Ireland. It is no wonder he believes the whole world revolves around him. Even if he didn't have autism (and associated beliefs of "I am an expert at everything! We will do everything that I want! I am the king of everything!"), we had so coddled him that at two and a half, the debut of another person and that other person's schedule must have been hard proof that he did not, in fact, run the world.

We knew we were ready for a second child. The fact that it took us a year to get pregnant with her made us all the more prepared. The evening after I delivered Grace, I waited for my husband to bring Noah into the recovery room. But with each minute, my anxiety mounted. I had done my research. I understood the kind of mammoth impact a new baby would have on Noah's understanding of the world and his place in it. Noah thrived on routine and uniformity. Would his universe implode when he caught sight of this red, squirming alien wrapped up like a burrito in hospital white?

In our first few months together, life was idyllic. That is, if you rule out a move, Matt's new job (with requisite traveling), and a nasty bout of the stomach flu. And did I mention that our new home was twenty minutes from anywhere? Our mail carrier didn't even arrive until 6:00 p.m., which is basically the next business day, so the way I figured it we paid for the view by being just about one whole day behind the rest of the world. It was for all of these reasons that Noah, Grace, and I spent many uninterrupted moments in that first year together, and why I had a ringside seat at the systematic destruction of Noah's one-man empire.

Grace did nothing but squeak, sleep, and nurse her first few weeks. She was like a puppy: cute enough to look at, but real boring after the first hour because she would fall back asleep. Noah would stick his head over the side of the bassinette each day expecting something new, but after a while he would move on. I could almost see the wheels turning: "This isn't so bad. She doesn't do anything."

In her third month, Grace was alert and smiling. Noah was suddenly interested again. This trend continued through to six months when Grace was sitting up and babbling to anyone who'd lend an ear. She was wearing pretty dresses and hair bows. She was mighty fun to play with, even for a boy. Noah grew to love her, nay, *obsess* over her. He would shove me out of the way to be the first one in her room. We would reach for the door handle simultaneously. "No, I do it," he would screech at me.

Noah and Grace would lie on the floor together under the mobile on the play mat, their pale hair touching. They would face each other on their bellies and Noah's face alone would make Grace explode with laughter. Noah loved her head. Her small, fuzzy, sweet-smelling head. He would pet it with the same uncontrolled intensity he also uses for his guinea pig. The same guinea pig I am afraid he's going to inadvertently choke to death.

But at this point in their idyllic relationship, Grace wasn't crawling yet. This was a critical distinction.

When Grace started to crawl at ten months, the dynamic between my children began to shift. Not dramatically, but in tiny, unobtrusive ways. Like the tiny way you get the whiff of something strange before you realize that the whole kitchen is on fire. Their interactions became even more charged when Grace started "cruising": that cherished time when babies learn to pull themselves up and move around furniture, and parents simultaneously realize that a playpen no longer cuts it because these locomotive little creatures have answered their life's calling to vanquish anything that chains, contains, or restrains them. They scuttle like cockroaches but are, alarmingly, twice as fast. Particularly when they're headed toward a set of unsecured stairs.

Not that I would know.

Noah didn't take kindly to this new mobility. Grace was now a threat. And it wasn't just his toys that were at stake. It was me. She demanded me with a pleading "MaMa" when she was wet, or teething, or it was Monday. She needed to eat when Noah did. And everything Noah had, Grace wanted. So Noah started to push her. At first, when we weren't looking; then, when we were right there warning him not to.

By Grace's first birthday, Noah's tactical maneuverings took a more aggressive turn. After one week of unsteady footing, she was racing around the house like a drunken sailor on bowlegged stilts. Noah followed her everywhere and wasn't just responding to a perceived peril. Now, he was taking the initiative to shut her down. He perfected the technique of sneaking up behind her and lowering his knees into her back so that she'd fall when he was already sprinting halfway across the room, claiming he didn't do it. The shoves multiplied, the toys flew. There were howls from both that curled my toes. Each day, I yelled, *"Gentle, Noah!"* somewhere between three and 57,000 times.

Gentle is not something my autistic son is capable of being. This is due largely to what experts call "mind blindness"— that inability to perceive other people's emotions or perspectives. To say his actions were hurting his infant sister meant nothing to Noah. Instead, he continued to shove her and repetitively, compulsively rub her downy head. When I asked him why he did it, he replied simply, "Because it's squishy. And it makes her scream." Ah, yes. Now it all makes sense.

Then one day, while I was overwhelmed with preparations for dinner guests (and while trying to keep up the facade of perfect domesticity), the tide of power turned. I was in the kitchen when Noah dogged Grace into the living room. He was an inch away at all times, half eager to be with her, half hoping he might find an empty floor register large enough to stuff her in. She was screeching. I was yelling, "Gentle, Noah!" and a skillet of chicken cacciatore was set to bubble over on the stove. I couldn't get to them so I yelled my directives, hoping to stop the fight I knew was brewing in the other room. Noah must have pushed Grace because I heard him make the guttural little snort he did when he tried to get momentum behind his hand. She screeched again. I yelled, "Gentle, Noah!" yet again, and mopped furiously at the tomato sauce on the floor. Because Grace didn't see me coming, she must have figured she was responsible for her own rescue. As I rounded the corner into the living room, I caught sight of them both on the floor. Grace's shrill cry became a howl, and as Noah's hand went up into her chest again, Grace opened her mouth so wide that I caught sight of two teeth coming in that I hadn't even known were there. She was desperate to get ahold of his hand, grabbing at his clothing, shaking her head from side to side in a frenzied attempt to latch on. In the one second she saw her opening, she pulled his hand to her mouth and bit down as hard as she could with razor-sharp puppy teeth.

From a combination of pain and outright surprise, he burst into tears, crying, "She *bit* me!" At this point, Grace had shuffled past me with a big smile and a "deedle deedle," and I had to stifle my laughter as I petted Noah's head and dried his tears. I explained that she'd finally had enough of his pushing. I told him again that he didn't need to push Grace to get my attention, but that nothing he did could ever make me stop loving him. I also explained, perhaps for the first time, something that would become a common refrain in our home: Noah had to always think about how his actions would make the person to whom they were directed feel. Though it was hard for him to understand, I told Noah that he was not the center of the universe, and that his kindness toward others would help them be kind to him too.

Still reeling from Grace's attack, Noah was sedate the rest of the night. In fact, he was most helpful when our dinner guests arrived, introducing himself, me, and my husband. And then he turned to Grace.

"And this is baby sister Grace. But be careful. She bites."

~

Into every family, a little sibling rivalry must fall. And fell it did. In buckets. After we had our third child, Jesse.

In our family, the days are hurly-burly, with much screaming, throwing, door slamming, hissing, puncturing, and wailing to accompany them. The children cannot be left to play on their own, nor even with each other. The multi-acre backyard is not big enough to control their skirmishing. Mealtimes, bath times, and bedtimes—when the children are necessarily gathered—become a thing to be dreaded.

Imagine then my distress when I discovered that not all families with children the same age as ours have to don flak jackets for a car ride. Imagine a shrill inner voice yelling, "Wait—what? It's not like this for everyone?!"

On a trip to the beach with our friends Rhonda and Jason, and their own three children, I looked over Noah's tear-soaked face to plead to my friend at dinner, "Why are your children so quiet?" She offered a few answers: "I'm a strict disciplinarian" (check); "I tell them public places require inside voices" (ditto); and "they lose privileges for poor behavior" (got it). I was heartbroken. I was doing all those things! Why couldn't I keep my children under control? What was wrong with me?

And then Noah had his first sleepover. We decided to take Grace and Jesse out to dinner. It was the quietest meal with children we had ever had. At home, the two played sweetly on the floor with each other. They went down for bed with nary a complaint. What was going on?

Though we struggled to admit it, Noah being gone was the difference. His nagging, his repetitive sounds, his theft of his siblings' toys, the compulsive rubbing of his brother's head, his inability to take turns—the ingredients of their altercations had themselves been altered. The patience of young children is of a shorter duration than that of their parents. We thereby deduced that when Noah taxes Mom and Dad to our limits, his brother and sister are already past the point of insanity.

"Gracie, say hmmm. Gracie, say hmmm. Gracie, say hmmm."

"Stop it, Noah!" Grace will howl in response.

This, on our ride to school.

"Jesse, give me the train! Bad Jesse, bad Jesse, bad Jesse!"

"Please, Noah!" Jesse begs in reply.

This, at home, after school.

Grace even made a point of petitioning the Lord during the most important prayer of her life. Sitting at the kitchen table after a seven-year-old Noah had given a five-year-old Grace the impassioned message of salvation and encouraged her to ask Jesus into her heart, the prayer was concluded with:

"And please let Noah stop bugging me."

These are not gentle power struggles. These are shrill battles of will with physical aggression involved. I could go on, but just recounting these stories makes me want a Xanax smoothie.

Noah is a walking dichotomy of defiance and compassion. He is tender but can be oppositional. He recognizes the appeal of community living, but as a kid with ASD, sometimes he cannot crack the code. Sometimes, fighting is the only way Noah knows to make a connection with someone else.

So much of teaching and parenting these kids on the spectrum is just simple tolerance for how they're wired. Which is so much a part of parenting kids of all types, really. "Make every effort to live in peace with everyone" (Heb. 12:14). I have preached this verse to my children ad nauseum. But peace is a rare visitor in our home. Discord, however, loves to pull up a chair and set its feet on the table. As parents, the responsibility to model peace lies with Matt and me. It starts with our own willingness to compromise, understand, and apologize. A certain gentleman learned this lesson the hard way when I told him to go back and apologize for something he said to a stranger a few days ago. I won't elaborate, but Matt, you know who you are.

Every one of our days involves a battle of sorts. We guide our children in the best direction we can, avoiding triggers (biological, sensory, fear-based), and create a reward system for when they make the correct choice. Sometimes the reward comes before the behavior and looks more like a bribe. Most importantly, we assert the value of an apology, particularly to the boys—something that doesn't come naturally to kids on the spectrum. There's that mind blindness again.

Sometimes, though, when we are very lucky, that apology does not have to be extracted, but comes of its own accord. Even if it arrives by virtue of repetition, by function of having seen the right thing modeled by someone else, it can feel like an unexpected gift. Like a few weeks ago, when Noah attacked his little brother for taking a LEGO off Noah's shelf. I was too tired to insist Noah apologize, but did manage to separate the two before pulling my bedraggled self back to the kitchen to finish making dinner. A few minutes later, I discovered this note at the entrance to Jesse's room:

"Jesse, I sorry. Here you go, good boy."

Underneath the note was one of Noah's favorite books, a gift to his brother.

Noah's tender note was all his own. It was totally, blessedly beyond my control or direction. From Noah's own heart sprung the impulse to apologize; from the Lord's own prompting came a message of love between two brothers.

My hands had been off the wheel. Too tired, I'd let go.

Miraculously, something wonderful had happened anyway.

~

I heard someone once say that the definition of insanity is doing the same thing over and over but expecting different results. Here's the thing: my sons are masters of repetition, of doing the same thing over and over again. Kids with high-functioning autism are often known by this characteristic. Repetition even fuels their relationships with others. Like siblings, for example. When Noah repeats nonsense in Grace's and Jesse's ears, continually pokes their legs, or regularly shoves their car seats, his siblings pretty much want to punch repetition in its face.

A few days ago, Matt and I sat on a bench in a TCBY with the kids and looked out the window to where a thin, smartly dressed mother sat with her two daughters. Two daughters that were younger than ours, and quieter than ours. They were in starchy, floral dresses with oversized bows; they sported tangle-free hair; and remarkably, they ate their frozen yogurt without missing their mouths so much as once. Where were these kids coming from? A babyGap ad shoot? I used to want to dress my kids like that, I thought. Now, all I want to do is find something that doesn't smell like a diaper full of rotting snails. But it was the *listening* that baffled me. This mother said "Stop," the kids stopped. The mom said, "Throw the rest away," and into the garbage can went the rest of their still-good scoops. I pressed my face longingly against the window.

Driving home that night, with a set of sugared little people screaming at each other at such a decibel that even the roar of the wind through open windows couldn't squelch it, I yelled, "Grace, if Noah's bugging you, just ignore him! It's not like you don't know how to do it—you do it to me *all the time!*"

Noah bugs Grace, Grace screams in protest.

Noah bugs Jesse, Jesse screams in protest.

Jesse bugs Grace, Grace screams at everyone. Partly because she's upset, partly because she likes to. Noah trained her from an early age that screaming is the best way to get attention. I beg them to stop. Torment, scream, reprimand, repeat. Last week in the car, Grace extended her leg to an overstimulated Noah, whispering, "You better not touch me," goading him so that when he touched her, she could scream at the top of her lungs and go on to repeat it. Multiple, multiple times. She is the middle child, the only girl, and the only neurotypical of my three. But I never need worry that her voice won't be heard. When she screams, I can hear the dogs at the dairy farm down the road howling. The only way to find a quiet place at our house is to be partially deaf or unconscious.

While I will never get perfect behavior from my children every time, I will encourage them to drive toward it anyway. In this way, how they fight with one another has to change. We expect it to. But maybe something also has to stay the same. As a mom, I have to keep doing what I'm doing *and* expect different results—even if they never come. Matt and I have already set the standard for our children. We ask them to toe the line whether they want to or are even capable of it. The sameness in our instruction is the parity to their repetitive behaviors. Noah and Jesse will probably always have to work harder than Grace to behave appropriately, but regardless of whether they ever change, our guidance mustn't.

I suppose this is a way of saying that the crazy must continue. Which makes sense, because every parent I know has to be just a little bit daft to be comfortable with all this mess.

~

There is an adage about the trail of "garbage" flowing from highest to lowest point. I will spare you the particular vernacular, good Christian woman that I am, but suffice it to say that there is a certain curse word involved which I'm pretty sure originated on *The Sopranos*.

From my beloved Noah flows much "garbage." As the oldest and most dominant of my children, he sets the tone of the whole house. But Noah has no idea that he holds this power because of that blasted mind blindness. He can remember the flavor of ice cream he ate three years ago when he was wearing the green T-shirt with the skateboard, but he cannot recall the repetitions of "Noah, you set the tone for the whole house! Please be kind!" Yeah, thanks, autism.

I realized this to a greater extent after we got a second dog. Our older family dog, Jackson, is too tired to fight Noah's molestations, like the tail-pulling or the attempts to ride him. Jackson is a Shiba Inu, which makes him approximately forty pounds and a mere eighteen inches high. The fact that this is an obvious trick-riding fail is somehow not obvious to Noah. God bless that dog. We've been spared many a trip to the emergency room by simple virtue of his advancing age and disinterest in fighting back. Similarly, our guinea pig is subjected to finger pokes through his cage while Noah grunts at him. I often open Noah's door to find Bubblegum high above Noah's head like the cub Simba in *The Lion King*. Noah believes he can talk to his guinea pig. But so far, Bubblegum's neglected to tell Noah to cut it with the acrobatics. The fish we once had escaped everything, what with that glass cube of a tank in which she lived. Noah hated the slime of her scales. Plus, we made sure the hole in the top was too small for Noah to get his hands through. The six hermit crabs miss all the poking by retreating into their shells, and the horses simply outsize Noah—a natural deterrent in itself.

However, our second dog was an Aussie Shepherd/Aussie Cattle Dog mix, and she has a different relationship with Noah altogether. Zelda *may* have been a bit of an impetuous acquisition around Valentine's Day (note: missing the littleness of holding a baby when yours are in grade school ought not to be satisfied with a spur-of-the-moment trip to the pet store because puppies, like babies, eventually grow up and can drive you insane). She was, according to Noah, the "Worst Valentine's Day present *ever!*" Unless one is prepared to have their children herded, one should think long and hard about a herding dog as a family pet. Zelda is prone to bursts of energy, tugs-of-war, and barking fits. I paid $250 for a dog trainer to spend the afternoon telling us how to handle her, and I want it all back. Particularly because her high-energy personality feeds Noah's aggression. Noah's heart is pure, his spirit is merciful. But his lack of empathy extends to both his siblings and his pets. When he was younger, Noah would wrap his hands around Zelda's throat and shove her to the ground with all the force he could muster. He would kick her and pull her ears and she'd come back for more with a wagging tail. God is to be thanked again for pairing us with a second good dog, because Zelda thinks it's all a game. She continues to lick her gratitude and love all over the face of anyone near her. My pleas to Noah that "It hurts her!" and "How would you feel if you were kicked?" were useless. I got the "I'm just playing, Mom!" or "I wouldn't like it if someone kicked me." They were the practiced answers that temporarily satisfied me. Then, when my back was turned, Noah was at it again. Just like he had been when he was shoving baby Grace onto the floor or squeezing little Jesse's fuzzy head.

Then, Noah entered a phase in which he would wind Zelda up in the hopes that she would clamp down on his arm. My son who flaps his arms also loves the squeezing pressure of her teeth on them. The sensory input of heavy teeth on his skin somehow grounds his spinning nerves by providing a sensation only mimicked by flapping. But it's only a matter of time before the wrestling starts hurting Noah, and he screams, "Get her off me!" Or "She's killing meeeeeeee!" Noah's grandparents and great-grandparents were theater people. It's more obvious at some times than others. Grace rivals Noah here in that every day is the "worst day of my liiiiiife!" These "worst days" are usually set off by something like a lost hair bow or the fact that McDonald's forgot the toy in her Happy Meal.

When he was big enough to interact with his siblings, large enough to move and think independently, my sweet, freckle-faced Jesse took on, for Noah, the role of the family dog. In Noah's economy, Jesse fell somewhere below Grace, but slightly above the guinea pigs. Now he too has learned to fight back, and what may once have been his go-along-to-get-along personality is now lost in his self-defensive dueling. We break up the boys like we break up our scrapping dogs. One has the other's neck, one is clutching the other's shirt. Teeth are involved. Sometimes they are dragging each other around the room. Two things have worked to provide us with some (short-lived) relief: pro-wrestling and a pillow.

My husband was raised in the era of Ricky Steamboat, when Gorgeous George was a household name and televised matches were the highlight of his male-dominated household. This isn't an interest he pushed on his boys. It arose of its own accord one day when Noah flipped through the TiVo and discovered a taped match that must have tapped some happy neuron in the lobe of his brain that deals with sensory perception. These men, flipping each other down onto a mat, fascinated him.

Jesse wandered into our room one day when Noah was spellbound in front of the television set. They sat like two pigeons on our footboard. The next night, with a new match playing in the background, the battle was under way. Noah slammed Jesse on the bed, Jesse parried with a headlock. I ran to separate them, but Matt stopped me.

"They're fine."

They were. For a moment. Until Noah decided to jump onto his prone brother, knees first, and my heart stopped.

"Enough!" I bellowed. That's when the pillow saved us, or, at least diminished by a considerable percentage the number of times I would have to discipline Noah for taking things too far.

The pillow itself was purchased for use by Matt and me, but never has something as simple as a pillow caused so much discord between spouses. The reason for the fight? That thing was solid as a stone wall. And neither one of us wanted it.

Prior to the wrestling incident, Matt and I had relinquished our sagging mattress to a memory foam bed. The promise of a good night's sleep and the backing of "doctors everywhere" persuaded us. We don't sleep nearly enough as it is, considering the constant interruptions from the night wanderings of tiny trolls, but we thought we might contribute better to the sleep we *were* getting by upping the mattress quality. Besides, we were forty. Isn't this what forty-year-olds did? We assumed a walk-in bathtub and a set of life-alerts were next. The bed cost us an arm and a leg. We might still not sleep as much, we thought, but at least we could sleep better. "For our health!" we reasoned.

In conjunction with this purchase, we were convinced by the saleswoman that the best accompaniment to our purchase was a set of memory foam pillows. These pillows came in a variety of firmnesses.

We both opted for "soft." Considering that you can't even jump on the bed without feeling like you've hit a wall, we decided we needed something with a little more give to it.

What came back from the factory was one "soft" pillow and one "suitable as a car jack" pillow. Wanting to wrap the process up and not wait for another pillow (patience not having ever been a virtue of mine), I told the salesperson, "Oh, it's no problem. I'll take that one!"

I'm kind and sacrificial like that. I beamed at Matt.

Matt was wary.

"Are you sure?" He tilted his head at me the way Zelda does. "We can just wait—"

"No. I'm good with this one! Promise!"

As it turns out, Matt had good reason to be suspicious. I had no idea what sleeping on that thing would actually be like. The first time I put my head down (or rather, let it drop too hastily), I told Matt I needed an Advil. I've hit open refrigerator doors and didn't hurt that much.

So began the struggle for pillow domination. With matching pillowcases, I could slip Matt's off his side of the bed and onto mine. Every time one of us slept on it, we woke up with back pain, neck pain, or cramped muscles. I had a good mind to call the company and tell them that whatever doctors were backing this memory foam stuff needed to spend a night on their own material and get their facts straight. But I didn't. I was chicken. Plus, I'd actually said I *wanted* the harder pillow. Like a fool. I wasn't about to admit defeat.

Matt, loving me, knowing I don't sleep well, and knowing that I am frequently sick, finally offered up the softer pillow to me for good. I was so touched that I promised not to use the hard one in a pillow fight against him anymore. The one and only time that had happened, Matt buckled to his knees. Every inch of his linebacker-sized frame.

From that point, Matt dumped the harder pillow onto the ground every night in order to get some sleep, retrieving one of the lumpy, old synthetic pillows from its place of retirement in the downstairs linen closet. But when he naps (which he loves to do—I am convinced he is part bear the way he loves to hibernate), he slides the soft pillow back to his side of the bed, and thus go the next ninety minutes or so because his sleep is so restful. As it should be, when you sleep on an unreasonably expensive pillow of any firmness.

So there, on the floor, the brick-solid pillow lay most nights. Until one day, I saw Noah pushing his fist into it.

"I like this."

Matt and I watched him.

"Yes, it looks like it."

"Can I have this pillow? Because if I do" (mashing his fists into it, folding it in half, kneeling on it) "I won't beat Jesse up as much." I didn't even care that he'd qualified his statement with "as much." I heard only the first part: "I won't beat Jesse up."

"Yes!" I leaped up. "Absolutely, honey! Let me get you a fresh pillowcase for it!"

I went flying down the hall. When I came back, I shot Matt a look. It was a look that said: "See? I get it! I get *him*!" As much as I will ever "get" him, I imagine. I get that he needs hard things, and tight things, and spaces into which to crawl. And doesn't like things that are sandy or gritty or itchy, and thrives on squeezing and tickling and getting mashed into the bed when Matt lays on him with all the poundage he possesses, per Noah's grinning request. So the pillow, moldable as a piece of clay, conforms every night to Noah's head—after he's had a good squeeze on it.

Jesse watches from his own bed, spared for now. Until Noah starts to complain the pillow is giving him a headache. Then, well. May God have mercy on our souls.

~

By function of the fact that we've held him back, Noah is the oldest in his class. He was at one time also the oldest in our neighborhood. Things are tricky when we have to remind our oldest—who comes with a bundle of nontypical challenges—to set a good example for the other kids. When the oldest one thinks differently from all the other ones, how do you tell him that what his brain is wired to do has to change? That he has to go from automatic to manual transition every time he makes a decision that involves other people? We start from the bottom up, and with the "least of these" (Matt. 25:40). We start with younger siblings, and even pets. We strive for righteousness in the care of all those entrusted to us. So our kids will go on being instructed in gentleness, kindness, and mindfulness. Even if—like Noah and Jesse—they don't always understand or remember how.

Matt and I have done what we can to control our children's boxing matches and insult hurling. We've tried to defuse statements like Noah's, made after he learned Jesse had broken something large in his absence: "Doesn't matter. I could still take him in a fistfight." We've tried to discourage statements like Jesse's, made when his older siblings were at Granny and Papa's: "I don't want them back! They have to live there now!" We try to derail proclamations like Grace's: "Mom, be honest. You love me more than the boys, don't you?" We have done it by modeling the appropriate behavior in the best way we can, and by giving each child a part of our time that they alone possess. Each one is encouraged and cuddled and taken on errands by themselves so that there is no perceived disparity in treatment. Because disparity in treatment is an entrée for discord. And it is also of the devil, I'm convinced.

This is the funnel for my control compulsion, also. Kind of a two-for-one. This is a time in my life where the strain of effort doesn't just lead to me running in circles or growing a migraine. I feel the Lord often remind me, "Sarah, set the best example possible for these three that I've given you. Set it with instruction and tolerance, the best you can, as often as you can." As often as I can? The best that I can? No problem, God. I'm super awesome at striving. Even when I feel like "I have no peace, no quietness; I have no rest, but only turmoil" (Job 3:26), I can keep on trucking, because I feel the weight of blessing in my arms when I hold them. I can see how very much the striving is worth it.

Turmoil is a part of the messy pursuit of parenting. The scrapping of my children continues of its own accord, and at a certain point my hands are tied. I can beg and plead and entreat my children to keep their grubby mitts off one another in the grocery store, but the ultimate decision to do so is up to them. Sometimes, no matter what we do, it will seem to my children as if they are in a battle. As it does to Grace, who proclaimed of late, "Mom, my life is boring because I have two brothers. I wish I had two sisters and just one brother. Then they would be outnumbered and I would win." Grace is also the one who, when asked what kind of face paint she wants at a carnival, always replies, "War paint." Because she is ready to fight. All the time.

These miniature people who showed up each in their own way, with their pieces put together in such lovely, unique mosaics; these hands that hold my own and my heart with it, they are so loved.

But they are loud in a way that only aircraft marshallers can appreciate, in part because two of the three are compelled by impulses that are difficult to control. It doesn't help that the middle one is, I'm convinced, half goblin. She is smart enough to be Svengali to the boys, and she doesn't even need a reward for motivation. I once heard her convince Noah that she would be his "servant" so that she could earn money to buy his video games out from under him. She is that good.

We have learned the only way through the mire of sibling antagonism is with an eye toward peaceful leadership, and the sheer determination to do it well, along with a blind faith that the Lord will take the chaos of us and make it something wonderful.

That, and a white noise machine so we can finally get some sleep.

5

I Get Paid for This, Right?

Unless the LORD builds the house,
    those who build it labor in vain.
Unless the LORD watches over the city,
    the watchman stays awake in vain.
It is in vain that you rise up early
    and go late to rest,
eating the bread of anxious toil;
    for he gives to his beloved sleep.

Psalm 127:1–2 ESV

Despite my haste to depart the law after contracting mononucleosis, I ultimately spent six years in private practice, first with the law firm, then in-house at an advertising agency. I left after having Noah because I was committed to the concept of dedicating my days to raising him and tending our house. There was a small part of me that thought, "Maybe this will be harder than I think." Yet I was madly in love with my son and couldn't bear the thought of our separation, so I quashed that idea and dove in.

I was right. It was harder than I thought. Way, way harder.

I also thought:

"I can't see the floor. There are six baskets of laundry on it."

"We have to order takeout, because I don't have the energy to cook and haven't set foot in a grocery store in a month. Also, I'm pretty sure I would forget Noah somewhere in the store."

"Sorry I look so gross, honey. I could only either nap or shower. I think you can guess what I chose."

"Oh, this? I think it's baby barf. It might also be frosting I ate from the can with a spoon yesterday."

Then there came this thought:

"I am a mother. I used to be a lawyer. Is being a mother 'enough'?"

My soul began another period of spinning unrest. My house didn't look clean enough, magazine-worthy enough, organized enough to justify what I'd done all day. Come to think of it, what had I done all day? As the kids grew, and I was out of my "I just had a baby so leave me alone" cocoon phase, I began to establish lists of tasks:

1. Organize all the baby books
2. Fold all the laundry
3. Grocery shop for the week and plan the weekly menus

4. Water all the plants and weed the garden
5. Take the dogs to the vet

This was Monday's list. No deviation permitted. Matt came home from work and I would barrage him with "Here's what I got done today . . ."

If I hadn't sliced through each item with a big red pen in an indication of total life domination, I would sulk the rest of the evening. Alternatively, I would work really hard at feeling guilty about what I hadn't done, while planning the next day's chores. Like this somehow completed another "task" on the list, even though it was psychological in nature.

"Honey, I only got two baskets of laundry done. Also, I worried really hard. So I can check that off."

At some point, I found that the kids were actually getting in the way of "getting things done." I had to prove accomplishment of something other than raising, playing with, being with these little people with their critical needs and imperative development. I mourn those days, those days of a driven need for justification. (Because who leaves a well-paying job only to raise their kids? One must raise their children, perfect the home, and maybe even take on a part-time job, right? I didn't permit the former alone to be enough for me, and if it was enough for my friends, they made it look like it wasn't by managing all domestic matters perfectly. Which just made things worse.)

Then one summer afternoon, Grace wanted to wear my high heels. I thought this was a thing that only happened in commercials for life insurance, where the little girl in soft focus wears high heels and a string of pearls, and is admiring herself in the mirror while someone in a soothing baritone talks about "taking care of her future." But my daughter was actually rifling through my closet for the highest, most impractical shoes she could find. Then, marching down the hallway in my shoes (and mastering them in better form than I have, which I find unsettling), she asked if she could paint her nails with a color she had pulled from under my bathroom sink. I told her no, that I had work to do and I couldn't oversee what I was sure was going to be a small disaster of spilled nail lacquer. She began to throw a fit.

Thinking there might be a suitable alternative, I asked if she wanted to wear some of my jewelry instead. She asked for my wedding rings.

Uh, no.

The fit was growing bigger.

Then Grace asked if she could wear the longest dress I own. I had visions of her careening down any one of a number of staircases in this house, propelled by five inches of aqua-colored patent leather heels. At this point, Grace was nearly apoplectic. No, no, no. I logically denied each request, but I was missing what was happening right in front of me. My daughter was trying to shape herself into her mother. Her mother who wears red fingernail polish on occasion, and loves her aqua-colored patent leather heels and the sundress that falls to the floor.

Grace wears glasses as I do. We have sat together at the optometrist, and she has asked, "Can you find me glasses that look like my mom's?" My daughter has requested haircuts like mine and loves horses like me. She has pulled from her drawers outfits that replicate what I am wearing.

This was the thing that I saw that day. I am a woman of certain roles that do not concern my daughter, that do not interest her. I am a lawyer and a housekeeper and a writer, but there has never been a day when I have seen Grace pretend to write a legal brief or fold a basket of laundry. I have instead seen her take on the physical part of me that is simply with her. The person who talks to her as she sits on the bed and asks her, "What dress do you think Mommy should wear tonight?" The person who says to her, "Come under the covers with me, little one, so we can snuggle," and then hears her little sigh, the one that tells me she is in her favorite place. The person who says, "I cannot wait for Saturday—that's our Mommy and Grace day!"

What my daughter sees is not what I polish and write and cook. Though in her own way she expresses appreciation for all of that. My daughter sees me, the simply present part. Grace sees a mother, above all. She sees not the "doing" part, but the "being" part.

She tells me by showing what part of me she appreciates the most.

To the crowd of parents for whom parenting comes easily: I salute you. You, of the Mommy and Me classes, with filled scrapbooks and handmade baby food. I took a Gymboree class with Noah when he was twelve months old and congratulated myself for a week. The closest I ever got to making baby food was mashing an overripe banana for Grace. I made a visit to my friend's house recently. She is an ICU nurse at a major hospital in Baltimore. She has two kids, an immaculate house, and the kindest, most complaisant children I've ever met. Her children are apparently drinking some magical elixir given to her by a genie. That's the best explanation I can come up with.

The children of the perfection-obsessed, mess-less parent are, I imagine, clean and obedient. They don't talk back. My five-year-old looked at me today and retorted, "Zip it, Mama!" I have a law degree. You'd think I'd be able to present him with a more convincing case for why this is inappropriate.

Though I might have once considered them the worthiest of endeavors, I do not sew my children's Halloween costumes, categorize their toys, or stencil their nursery walls. Instead, I write an article about peace in the home, and then later yell at my children in the backyard, pleading with them to stop because "all the neighbors can hear you!" Subsequently, I terrorize their motorized car with a whiffle bat because the battery-powered siren won't shut up, thereby drawing even more attention to the spectacle behind our house. Sometimes, I run three kids out the door in the morning and find myself at the grocery store before I realize I haven't brushed my teeth. I buy a lot of mints.

I gave up a position in the corporate world to stay home with my children and would retake the bar exam in a minute flat if I could negotiate with God on lightening my current workload. "Please, Lord, just today, let them do what I ask the first time, without threats, pleas, or bargains." Parenting is work. And not the "I'll meet you at the office happy hour" kind of work. Not the "I need to get this report done because my boss is gonna be corked" kind of work. It's the "if I don't get dinner on the table right now, someone is going to have a meltdown, and then there's a pretty good chance something will get thrown at me" kind of work.

This parenting business is tricky, sticky, exhausting, and inscrutable. I wing it every day. I have given up on parenting manuals because of conflicting advice between sources and the sheer force it takes to finish reading a book in less than a year. I occasionally catch a few minutes of *The Nanny*, and that's all it takes to convince me I've already dropped the ball. I'm not always able to muster the appropriate follow-through with discipline. Especially not with two of our three on the warpath approximately forty-eight out of every sixty consecutive minutes. "Time outs" can sometimes be more like "I'm only disciplining you if you can get up and walk yourself over to the mat for me."

Thank God for Matt. Because I can be more observant than he (this is attributable to the second set of mother eyes we get after childbirth, including those in the back of my head, which, when I used the phrase with Noah—literal as he is—terrified him so that he dug under my hair for a full minute, thinking he'd find them), I do better to catch poor behavior and initiate discipline. Matt does better on the follow-through. Then together, we talk to the perpetrator about why s/he is being disciplined, and how the behavior needs to change. I don't know if it's the best possible system, but I know that our kids are not permitted to run wild. Actions have consequences in our home, both good and bad. No one escapes this maxim.

Which is why the hair on your neck stands straight up when you read something like this:

In 99 out of 100 cases, an autistic kid is "a brat who hasn't been told to cut the act out. . . . They don't have a father around to tell them, 'Don't act like a moron. You'll get nowhere in life.' . . . [They should be told,] 'Straighten up. Act like a man. Don't sit there crying and screaming, idiot.'"[1] Oh that this radio commentator had a window into our daily life. If "curing" autism was as easy as telling someone to behave correctly, we'd have won a national title by now. That kind of statement also assumes there is no father around here telling people not to act like morons. But there is, and he does. In Christian love, of course.

I'll tell you what parenting feels like most of the time: a power struggle. It's the struggle in a public place between you and your overloaded son. It's the quiet struggle between your own inner critic and the barely audible "tsk-tsk" of the woman two booths over at the pizza joint, or the microphone jockey who thinks instead of a developmental disability, what your son actually has is a case of poor parenting. It's the struggle between you and your husband on the best way to handle a conflict between your children, or the struggle between the will and the mind, when the will wants to pull the covers over her unwashed hair, and all the mind can think is, "The critical task of raising these kids must be undertaken well!" Also, the mind thinks, "Matt is going to have to use a spackling knife to pry me out of bed if I stay here any longer." But mostly, it thinks of raising the kids well.

Our oldest dog, Jackson, decided to pee on Jesse's elaborate firefighter setup recently, including ten fire trucks he'd arranged in a neat row. I'm not sure how the dog, low to the ground as he is, sprayed it all so effectively.

Said Jesse: "Mom, can you do me a solid and clean that up?"

Said Mom: "I tell you what. You can do me a solid and throw them in the trash can, then, because I'm not cleaning this up without some help."

Either the burdens of motherhood are obvious, or I suck at hiding them. Because Grace told me a few weeks ago that she wants to be a mother, but without the kids part because they were too much work. To which I replied, "Well, don't you know that I love you?" Reply: "Yes, but sometimes you yell at me." To which I could have added, "I also sometimes send you to school in the pants you wore yesterday, and silently hope you'll quit riding lessons so we can save some money," but I bit my tongue.

There was a guitar once, in this house. It had been given to Noah as a gift for his birthday some years ago. But that didn't prevent him one night from putting his foot through the center and crushing it to pieces. We ask him to feed the dogs and let them out, and he wails like he's been caught in a wood chipper. He can't pick his clothes up off the floor without grunting and hissing his complaints—when he actually follows through with our request. He hits his siblings without distinction—pushing and kicking before his mind has even caught up with his body. The soft-skinned, grinning toddler whose hand he once let me hold is now always ready to throw down. Even the dogs get it. And when he's out of the house? We can practically hear the angels singing.

This is hard to believe for those who know Noah on the "outside." "He is so sweet," they croon, "so polite and compliant and kind." Yes, he is. I have always known that his heart is tender and good. But even now, at school, he is asserting himself to the point of being disruptive with his "loud interruptions." Brain and body are not in accord.

What's more is that Matt and I feel like we get the dregs of his behavior. He will eventually cave to his teacher's will. The pressure to be "good" is stronger at school among his peers, because along with a bunch of other things, Noah's inherited his mother's deferential personality that makes public shame feel like a firing squad. However, it's a fight to the finish at home. There are tears and screams and gnashing of teeth. "Oppositional defiance disorder" returns again to mind. As many kids with ASD do, he feels the need to assert himself over anyone who doesn't share his perspective or desires. I came to the conclusion this week that he tasks himself so hard with obedience in public places (for fear of embarrassment) that there is nothing left when he comes home to us. He's frayed at the edges from holding it all in.

When it comes right down to it, I lack the power for any of this parenting business. I am but a vapor in the wind, a mist (James 4:14). It stands to reason I can't do a thing without power from another Source: the Maker of the mist, this failing body.

"I also pray that you will understand the incredible greatness of God's power for us who believe him" (Eph. 1:19 NLT). Power for parenting's workload; the power to see it through, and well. We need it every day.

~

In Vilas County, a small area at the top of Wisconsin's mitten shape, populated more by musky fish and eagle than by humans, there is a cabin. This cabin sits on Lake Mani-towish, which is mostly clear and always cold. The craw-fish scoot across the lake's bottom, the evergreens line its shores. I spent a portion of every childhood summer with my brothers and sister at this cabin, the four of us separated at bedtime by only a folding pocket door through which we whispered jokes and threats and "I'm telling Dad!" The seven-hour drive from our Waukesha, Wisconsin, home to this cabin, undertaken every summer, must have been its own form of work for my beleaguered parents, particularly in the pre-tablet, pre-gaming-system, pre-DVD-player-in-the-car days. My grandparents owned this modest rancher, and after my grandmother died, her memorial service was held there.

So it was probably for this reason that after she died, I dreamt about my grandmother at this cabin. Seldom do I have a dream that years later I can recall with clarity enough to write about it, but mine went like this:

My grandmother and I were standing opposite the cabin, on the small inlet island that now houses her ashes in its shallow earth. The sun was to our faces, streaking down through hundreds of pine trees, and Lake Manitowish stretched out before us, smooth as a dinner platter. We were raking with gap-pronged rakes—rakes with spaces too wide to keep anything between them. There were so many trees, and the prongs were so far apart, that all we succeeded in doing was moving the evergreen needles around a bit. We were raking for nothing. It wasn't getting us anywhere. I remember tension wafting upward, my sense of agitation increasing because we weren't accomplishing anything visible. But my grandmother laughed and kept on raking, nudging me without a word to do the same.

That's sometimes what this path feels like. That movement-going-nowhere feeling, finding myself breathless at the sheer volume of what needs to be done, thinking I am raking the first of a million pine needles with a broken rake.

To therapy. Again.

"To the time-out mat, Noah!"

"Here, let me show you again how to button a shirt."

"Yes, he has autism . . . Yes, I know he looks 'normal.'"

"*How* much did his psyche evaluation cost?"

"There is no sand in your sandwich! I promise. How do I know? Because I made it!"

"How many times do I have to tell you to pick your clothes up off the floor?"

Raking, raking, and more raking; raking even on days when I stop my complaining long enough to look around, and thank God in humility for their relative ease. We have the verbal spectrum kids—the ones who like to make new friends and, save for some well-modified behaviors, don't look anything other than a bit "odd." They aren't the ones spinning plates in the corner or pointing to flashcards to tell us what they want for dinner. Which is precisely why I sometimes want to call it all off. Because I think this is as good as it gets.

"That's it!" I sometimes want to yell. "No more work trying to make them more functional!"

It makes a body tired, thinking of what a marathon these hidden disabilities of theirs are. This past Christmas taxed us to our limits. The lights, the sounds, the late nights, the sugar, the break from routine—these are the nitroglycerin of an ASD kid's world. I was glad to have the whole thing behind us. This isn't a sentiment of which I'm terribly proud.

"Joy to the world, the Lord has come."

Now, can we get the tree packed up?

I thought about raking this morning when I woke, and how our path with our children—neurotypical and otherwise—is really no different than that of the average parent's journey with the average child of an average age and gender. There is a lot of daily tending required. Child-rearing is an undertaking of lifetime maintenance. It is exhausting for even the saintliest of parents. Our family just happens to have a few extra pounds to carry on the journey.

Child-rearing is also a task of many unseen moments, when it's just you and your child, and there's nothing to prove but everything to lose in the opportunity to do the raising well. It's only when your two-year-old decides on a battle of the wills in the vet's office when you're waiting for your cranky dog's abscessed face to be examined at close range that the way in which you parent *really* takes center stage. But the Lord's vision never fails. His eye is ever on us. He sees what is done in secret, and rewards it (Matt. 6:6). My reward is my children: my bespectacled Grace and her "seven kisses," my daredevil Jesse and his thumb-sucking embraces, and my Noah, the one who makes it all so hard and so easy at the same time, the one who, as the oldest and most "visible" in this combination of things the Lord had seen fit to visit upon him, alters the course of our family and its dynamics, but who, with characteristic (and likely unconscious) nonchalance said to me this morning, "I know, I know. I'm the best little boy ever, right?"

Right.

⁓

It was a moment in which I was conscious of the words coming out of my mouth, their very shape and feel, but like rivulets of oil in a lake, they were impossible to control once they started flowing.

"Oh Noah, just *shut up!*"

"Shut up" is a no-no in our house. As is "hate," "stupid," all manner of body part reference, and potty humor. But I as the mother, tasked with teaching my children the right way to speak and be, had not only used a forbidden phrase at Noah, I'd screamed it at him during one of his, as we call them, "autistic moments."

In the haste of our Sunday morning rituals and in an attempt to get to church on time, Noah made his siblings breakfast. "Made" is to be interpreted loosely here. "Placing" might be a better verb. As in "placing" a banana on a plate. But it was a win. We were touched by his kindness toward his brother and sister. However, we learned too late that he hadn't fed himself.

I'll pause momentarily to say that on any given day, we've got about 50 percent of the autism struggles managed with the boys. Here, the first 50 percent was compassion, which Noah exhibited freely and without being prompted. Fantastic! However, the second 50 percent was executive functioning and self-care. He hadn't remembered to feed himself. Assuming everyone had eaten, I started barking dressing orders for church. Noah started whining. Loudly.

"But I haven't even eaten yet!"

"Wait, Noah—didn't you just eat a banana?"

"Yes, but no one made *me* breakfast!"

"Well, can't you just grab a Pop-Tart for yourself like you did for Grace and Jesse?"

"Mom, no! Dad promised me eggs! And I don't have anything to eat! And I don't want a Pop-Tart!"

"Fine, Noah. I will make you some breakfast."

(Pause for five minutes, wherein I scrambled eggs, heated Toaster Strudels, and poured juice.)

"There you go, honey."

"Mom, no! You didn't let me put the icing on the Toaster Strudels myself the way I like to!"

"Oh Noah, *please just shut up!*"

Whereupon Noah's eyes welled up, his mouth took an upside-down horseshoe shape, and he tore from the kitchen up into his bedroom where he slammed the door.

That is how we began the Lord's Day.

Though late (with all that rushing and yelling coming to naught), we made it to church. And a good thing too. Because after all that, we needed some church. I could practically feel the Lord sitting next to me when our pastor put the message on the screen. As part of the "Culture of Honor" series he was teaching (living as those made alive in Christ), the day's message was from Colossians chapter 3, particularly, bearing with one another and forgiving one another as Christ has forgiven us. For added applicability, there was Colossians 3:21: "Fathers [or parents], do not embitter your children, or they will become discouraged."

Thanks for the sledgehammer, Lord.

The first thing I was going to do when I saw Noah come out of Sunday school was get on my knees and ask him to forgive me because I knew I had discouraged him. That is exactly what I did. He responded exactly as I knew he would: with grace and compassion that I didn't deserve.

"Oh Mom, I know you're sorry. It's OK. I forgive you."

I so often lose sight of Noah's unique construction when I am with him because the line between "typical" and "atypical" has begun to blur. Many years of therapies, an early diagnosis, and our proactivity in getting him treatment has made for a wonderfully functional young man with a hard-to-detect autism spectrum diagnosis. What a blessing. But I so often forget the way he's wired that when he melts down because no one has "made" him breakfast, or made it the "right way," I'm quicker with judgment than mercy.

I asked him later why he had been so upset that morning.

"I thought no one would remember to feed me."

What did my mother's heart actually hear?

"I was afraid I would go hungry."

My anxious son finds a worry around every corner.

So I told him, "No matter what happens, I will make sure you never have to go hungry. That must have been a scary feeling for you, but Mommy and Daddy love you. You are a treasure, and we have promised the Lord to honor and take care of you. I don't want you to worry about having enough to eat ever again."

Matt must have heard the same thing. Because after I let him make the grocery run for this week, after trip upon trip from the car to the kitchen counter with endless bags of food, my husband, he who harbors a silent anxiety himself about our refrigerator not being full to overflowing, slipped the receipt onto the table.

The next thing I remember is Grace splashing water on my face, helping me come to.

~

You know that moment when you take your jeans out of the dryer and they're just a little snug? That unhappy moment between panicking that you've hit the pasta too hard and that little bit of time before they re-conform to your shape and stretch a smidge? I attempted mine a few months ago during a period of particular challenges in my life, huffing and shifting these "everyday" jeans (read: *not* my "fat jeans") up my legs, until they'd reached my waist. But I was unable to button them. "They'll stretch," I reassured myself. "Just walk around without buttoning them," I said. Brilliant, I thought. That'll open them up. Only it didn't. After fifteen minutes of wearing them barely hitched over my hips, I had to lay on the bed and enact every romantic-comedy cliché by sucking in and zipping up at the same time. I had gotten them on all right. But I couldn't bend over because I was afraid of what might come spilling out.

Why the sudden costuming difficulty? The sudden change in girth? Because I was eating everything I could get my hands on. I had reached the tragic intersection of slowed metabolism and a newly acquired tendency to stress eat. At that particular juncture in my life, the world's many earnest burdens included an out-of-work husband, a sick son, and a daughter whose new diagnosis of amblyopia frightened her, as Grace thought the patch she had to wear over one eye would make her look like a pirate, but not the cool kind.

In the month of the jean debacle, breakfast was looking like two bagels: one, a bagel sandwich with egg, sausage, and cheese, the other, a bagel with honey, orange, and cranberry cream cheese that Jesse didn't want. Impressively, that had followed half a chocolate donut at my kids' "breakfast with parents" event. Normally, the vainer part of me would have demurred at the thick, sugary donuts (who wants to be the one stuffing in the simple carbs when all the other moms are sipping coffee and snacking on apples?), but I folded halfway through. There is no ladylike way to eat a frosted donut, by the way. I discovered this by waiting too long to check my face after everyone had left the cafeteria.

Please, people. Be a friend, and wipe a face.

I used to be a stress shopper. Oh how I loved stress shopping. No extra calories. No guilt. No self-flagellation or moaning in bed after a too-big dinner. I had an extensive wardrobe for a much smaller body frame. But we don't have the money for that anymore. So I had turned to food. And not just the sugar that once brought me comfort (sugar's a natural choice for me—there's a correlation between sugar and anxiety, as sugar stimulates the same neural pathways that promote euphoria and relaxation). Some nights are an Italian bonanza: wine, cheese, and salami before dinner, then two pieces of French bread and a huge bowl of sausage and marinara rigatoni. For dessert? Reese's chocolate peanut butter cups. This was an actual meal. I didn't even know my stomach had that kind of room. (Guess what? It doesn't.)

Some days, the joy amidst the work of this lifetime parenting project proves hard to unearth. I am learning to see it, though, when the scale of my life decreases, when the small things are observed on the level of the little people to whom my life is dedicated. My ear lowered down to where my children speak their wonderful things helps me hear Noah when he tells me that the rigatoni I made for dinner is "the best thing" he's ever eaten. This amazes me, as it's nowhere close to the Asian dumplings, pinched, folded, and steamed from scratch that were, I thought, the hallmark of a good wife. It is just something made easily, that makes my son happy with similar ease. And when we both eat too much of it, we can laugh about how we're set to burst.

I find added joy in the candle Grace helped me pick out, and how she squealed, "Ooh Mom! Smell this," when she did. I love the flicker of its little light in the still-dark morning kitchen, and she does too. Because she is always up before the sun and there to see it. I find joy in Jesse's yelling from the other room, "A squirrel! A squirrel!" because to be as excited about anything as my son is about a rodent with a chestnut is a great joy, indeed. I find joy in the smell of bleach on a basket of white, fluffy towels because it means I have gotten the laundry done. Or, some of it.

I find joy in Noah's math test that comes home requiring a signature. For though he scored a 78 percent, his answer to a story problem requiring him to show his work was answered thusly:

"I thought to myself and BAM! It's in my head."

Which made me laugh so hard it shook the belly in my too-tight jeans.

"I'm going outside!" Noah will shout to me from the stairs. But before I can tell him to wait for me and to put on a heavier jacket and shoes other than his Crocs, he is gone, flying outside in a whirl of limbs that he's trained for maladroit propulsion. I thank the Lord that we live in the country, on an elevation high enough that I can see him racing from most spots in this place. There he goes—Noah, my escapist. The one who leaps without looking, who never counts the cost.

My daughter Grace also regularly takes her life into her own hands, but I watch her measure distances, adjust strides, push back her glasses with a forefinger, and make her move. But Noah and Jesse, who are both possessed of enough fear and anxiety for any adult (let alone a child), paradoxically skate the razor's edge the minute they see it without any calculation whatsoever. They leap, wander, hide. They are fascinated with the thought of death ("What happens to the body?" "Does it hurt?" "When do the smells start?"), but they cannot comprehend how their actions might hasten it. Those two are oblivious to danger, ignorant of their own mortality. This is one of the more subtle but common manifestations of autism.[2] I have a number of small heart attacks each day.

Last year at a friend's birthday pool party, Noah believed he could swim when he could not. He complained about his life vest as I was setting out our towels. In the single instant at which my back was turned to him, he tore off his vest and jumped into water that was just six inches too deep. Under the smooth surface of the pool, I saw his eyes wide with terror. I will never forget the look on his face. I pray I will never see that look again. With one step, I reached down and tore him from the water.

114

I'd love to say Noah was "scared straight" by his near-drowning, but a similar event occurred only a few weeks later. For Noah, the laws of physics, medicine, and human psychology apply only if he agrees with them. Only if he agrees to live by them. If Noah believes he can swim, it doesn't matter to Noah that he cannot.

I have pages of stories on Noah's elopement: the day his foolish young mother attempted an outing with him and his new baby sister to the zoo on a summer day, only to have him dart from her into a packed gift shop where he remained for ten horrifying minutes; his tendency to hide in the basement, behind the hedges, down the street in a neighbor's car; his sprinting across crowded parking lots, his darting unaccompanied out of reach at a crowded fair, or his race-and-leap into the nearest pool. Our friend and former neighbor Karen recalls with latent anxiety the time she was watching Noah and he decided on a unilateral game of hide-and-seek. He chose her large SUV to hide in and didn't tell her where he was going. She called us in a panic after a few minutes, telling us she had turned her back in the kitchen, and he was gone. While on the phone with us in her driveway, Noah jumped out of the car and yelled, "Surprise!" We all breathed a sigh of relief, but despite his wide, self-impressed grin, we told Noah it wasn't funny to anyone but him.

As this past cold New Year dawned, I was lying in bed, willing myself not to hear the yelling and scuffling down the hall. Matt was still sleeping, mouth agape. Once again, my husband's skill of impenetrable sleep was on full display. Matt can also turn off his hearing at will. The deep sleeping and selective deafness must both stem from the same neurological pathway in his brain—the one that lets him not hear kids outside his door though they're hollering at each other in full voice.

I, on the other hand, have mother ears. The kind that let you hear your crying child at the end of the hall, through two closed doors, over the hum of a box fan, in the middle of the night. So over the growing din of that morning, I heard a little hiss of something over the carpet, attended by a tiny crackle of paper.

The kids were sending us notes again, I thought. And then I threw a pillow over my face and pretended it was still only four in the morning and I had a few more hours to sleep.

When Matt and I finally uprooted ourselves from the bed approximately 20 minutes later, I found, as I had suspected there would be, a note at the bottom of our bedroom door. It read:

> Dear Mom and Dad, I have ran away from home. Sign Noah

Are you kidding me? I'm only seven hours into the New Year!

I bolted past Grace and Jesse in the hallway, screaming, "Where is your brother? Where is Noah?" I yanked open the front door as I shoved my feet into a pair of boots, scanning the neighborhood for something that resembled a little boy. Then I turned back into the house, and ran to the basement door, pulling a coat on over my pajamas at the same time. Flinging the door open, I yelled down the stairs, "Noah!"

That was when he jumped out from behind the couch screaming, "Surprise!"

I collapsed over the back of the sofa and put my head in my hands.

The time between reading the note and startling when Noah jumped out couldn't have been more than sixty seconds. But a minute of suspended heart rhythm, a minute of horror seizing the gut, a minute of "what do I do next?" is a minute too long. It was a minute that probably took six months off my life on the back end.

I was panting, doubled over in the living room. Noah trotted over with his trademark gap-toothed grin. He had no concept of why I was worried.

"Noah! Why did you write that note? I don't understand . . ."

"'Cuz I was foolin' ya!" (Noah's regular comedic fare isn't always "funny" in the traditional sense. For example: "Mom, let's make a huge batch of cookies with gluten and then tell everyone they're gluten-free!" Or, "Surprise!" screamed at full volume when your terror has reached its upper limits, and you're convinced you'll have to call the police and later explain to them you can't manage to keep an eye on your own children.)

He was just "fooling" me into thinking he'd left me forever. I thought again of how when Grace and Jesse were tottering infants, Noah would compulsively rub their heads because (1) they were "squishy," and (2) because it made them scream and he "liked it."

That mind blindness of his is a real $&%*@!

"Peace I leave with you; my peace I give to you. Not as the world gives do I give to you. Let not your hearts be troubled, neither let them be afraid" (John 14:27 ESV).

I felt the Lord take a seat on the couch next to me. I was so peeved, and still so scared, that I didn't want to hear Him. But He was going to be heard. Like always.

"Hey there."

Still shaking with fear, still somewhere in my mind believing that Noah had truly vanished, I didn't respond.

"Listen, Sarah. Don't let your heart be afraid when you think your son has disappeared, but instead, remind him (yes, I know you've done it before, but it may take a few thousand times) of what other people could be feeling as a result of his actions. He has to know why you were afraid. He doesn't understand why. Instruct him on principles of safety and awareness (yes, I know you've done this too, but keep going).

"You're still anxious. Don't be [Matt. 6:31]. Tap into the power, the love, and the sound, capable mind I gave you [2 Tim. 1:7]. You're already figuring out the best ways to approach parenting as your children grow. I know how scary this venture is. But you have to trust Me with Noah. With all of them."

"I'm trying, Lord!" I insisted during our internal dialogue. "But I can't seem to unknot the fear in my gut whenever I take Noah to a public place. Or when the doorbell rings. Or when the weather is nice and he wants to run outside. Or when we're headed to the beach, or the pool, or anywhere, really, because, God, You have to understand—I can't bear the thought of losing one of my children!"

Here, the Lord paused for emphasis, waiting until my panicked sheep voice shut up and I could actually hear Him.

"You remember I know how that feels, right?

"Child, I gave Noah to you. Don't you think I've got him covered [Ps. 91:4]? Putting your trust in Me means you're safe. And so is Noah [Prov. 29:25]. So are all of them. But you know, honey, a few dead bolts probably aren't a bad idea.

"Now, go and get your rake. There's work to be done."

So I did. And I will, tomorrow and every day thereafter. I will wear a smile on my weary face. For the work itself is pure joy, and the rewards are more than abundant.

6

Sandy Sandwiches, or How to Be Embarrassed in Public without Even Trying

May the LORD now show you kindness and faithfulness, and I too will show you the same favor because you have done this.

2 Samuel 2:6

Kids are embarrassing. They throw fits in Olive Garden before the breadsticks show up and then you have to wonder how you're going to get through the rest of dinner without shoving a napkin in their screaming mouths. They help themselves to the Nilla Wafers in the grocery cart before you've made it to the checkout, forcing you to laugh nervously at the checkout girl and try to brush the crumbs off the conveyor belt while she puts the empty box back together just to scan it, throw it in the trash, and give you a dirty look. They just so happen, on the day you've hired a babysitter, to decide that they have a future career in art, and the medium they love most is poop, and the canvas they have closest is their crib so that when the sitter comes to retrieve them from their nap, the nursery room looks like something out of *A Clockwork Orange*.

Now add to all that embarrassment a form of neurobiology that really turns up the volume on public humiliation. This type of public humiliation, for example: when your eldest son barfs in a crowded Outback Steakhouse because he thinks there is something in his burger, despite your herky-jerky attempts to circumvent his reaction by using one tactic after another:

"No, Noah, the burger is perfect. Here, I will take a bite." (*son gags*)

"Here, switch with me. You can have my salad." (*son gags again*)

"Noah, look closely at the applesauce. There isn't any dirt in it. Watch Mommy take a bite." (*son gags, gags, gags, baaaarfs!*)

I am happy to report incremental progress in this regard. While applesauce, diced pears, rice, couscous, strawberry jelly, and other foods of a "gritty" consistency may always be off limits, my son has happily announced that he can now eat with my neighbor's (normally barefoot) baby in the room. I didn't ask him why, but if I had to guess, I'd say it's because she's old enough to finally be wearing shoes. Which also means she's old enough to cover those repugnant, naked feet. Which further means a slice of pizza can be eaten without the usual encore of barf-cleaning or gag-aversion.

Our family's "flavor" of autism is not the head-banging kind, but the "Why is that lady so fat?" in a crowded grocery store kind. It is the breathing in someone's face while they speak because he has no concept of personal space kind. The kind we have is a challenge in its own right, different from those of other children on the spectrum because my children look so "normal." Which is why the things that come out of their little bodies and mouths can leave spectators with their jaws on the floor. Social obtrusion in a child with a hidden disability leaves plenty of room for parental criticism ("why can't you control that kid?"). Which can sometimes feel like quite a slap in the face. There are things said and done by these kids of ours that have left us red-cheeked and stammering on more than one occasion.

Last year, Noah and I were sitting alone at the back of the deli we frequented during our Tuesday night karate/gymnastics run. Karate was part of our strategy to let our children explore the things that interested them. So far, we've been through soccer, karate, gymnastics, football, lacrosse, and horseback riding. I'll decline to guess how much all these passing fancies have cost us, but we have set a rule that our children must see each project through to the end of a season. So on that particular day, Grace was vaulting herself into the air across town. Matt was getting Jesse a haircut next door. ("Haircut" was, in this instance, loose vernacular for "hair shave," as despite Matt's explicit instructions, the "stylist"—again, using the loosest of vernacular—ignored his instructions, and took a pair of clippers to Jesse's whole head. (Think *Full Metal Jacket* on a thirty-six-pound frame.) I was relishing the quiet conversation with Noah, whose manner of speech generally falls to one of two extremes: harbinger of a verbal onslaught or taciturn observer sworn to silence. That particular night, he was the former.

"And then we did flying side kicks, and I have a belt test on Saturday, Mom, so don't forget, and I got there in just enough time to spar with a girl that I haven't met before, and then there was another kid that I took down on the first try—"

Then his face scrunched up. He pressed his eyes closed, and his mouth made a crinkled O.

He lowered his voice. "Mom, my tummy hurts."

"Well, honey, you just chugged twenty ounces of Powerade. Do you think it has something to do with that?"

"Probably." And then he was right back to shoving macaroni and cheese in his mouth. "Where did Dad take Jesse? To Hair Cuttery, or the new place? What kind of haircut is he getting? Is he going to come back here or—"

There was the pained face again. Noah is normally "ticky" at dinner anyway, having spent the total of his self-control reserves at school, and having to process sights, smells, sounds, and tastes simultaneously. That means at dinner, when he is able to let down, he gives in to impulses like face-making and finger-flicking, or standing and rocking. But on that night, there was something else going on with the face he was making.

"Ooh Mom. My stomach is just *killing* me!" His voice was getting louder. I heard the intensity in his voice and feared that a scene was coming. Thankfully, the bathroom was just a few steps away. I suggested he visit it.

He was out of his seat then, pacing. "I don't know, Mom, I don't know."

Noah has certain bathroom "oddities." For example, he will not perform a certain bodily function anywhere but our bathroom. Additionally, Noah will only perform said act fully unclothed, George Costanza style, naked as the day he was born. Here is Noah's intensity, intensified. When our bathroom is unavailable, he has been known to hold up a port-o-pot line at an outdoor festival because re-dressing oneself is hard in a noxious six-foot cube, and it's even harder in the summer heat when a line of un-sober partygoers is telling you to hurry up.

At this point, Noah was truly beside himself. "Oh Mom, oh Mom! You gotta help me!" He flew into the bathroom and left me alone at the table. Help him with what? I scanned the room, like there was a clue somewhere that I had missed. Noah was out just a moment later. "Mom! I need you to come in here! Please, please!"

I glanced up at the men's restroom sign, and back at my son, and tried to explain—quickly and efficiently—that because our "hardware" is different, I'm not allowed to go into the men's bathroom, and to do so could make for both an awkward situation and a possible misdemeanor. I told him I would be able to talk to him through the door, but had to stay outside.

The explanation didn't satisfy him. He was very nearly yelling now. "Mom, please! You have to come in and help me!" I was getting stares from other tables.

OK, mother-conscience. It's go time.

I remembered a story that had moved me once, something that had made my heart race in that space between anger and compassion because of who had been hurt, and who had failed to help the hurting.

"A man was going down from Jerusalem to Jericho, when he was attacked by robbers. They stripped him of his clothes, beat him and went away, leaving him half dead. A priest happened to be going down the same road, and when he saw the man, he passed by on the other side. So too, a Levite, when he came to the place and saw him, passed by on the other side. But a Samaritan, as he traveled, came where the man was; and when he saw him, he took pity on him. He went to him and bandaged his wounds, pouring on oil and wine. Then he put the man on his own donkey, brought him to an inn and took care of him. The next day he took out two denarii and gave them to the innkeeper. 'Look after him,' he said, 'and when I return, I will reimburse you for any extra expense you may have.'

"Which of these three do you think was a neighbor to the man who fell into the hands of robbers?"

The expert in the law replied, "The one who had mercy on him."

Jesus told him, "Go and do likewise." (Luke 10:30–37)

I ran to the door of the restroom and cracked it open (to what was, I'm sure, the certain dismay from the tables behind me), announced my presence, and entered. Noah was in the back stall, crying and tugging on the handle because he couldn't get the door shut. I suddenly realized his dilemma—he was in too much pain, and too embarrassed to ask for help with something specific. In his panic, all he could communicate was "help." He is able to utter so many wonderful words in such long chains of beautiful thought. And yet sometimes he cannot figure out how to say the simplest thing, like what it is he needs help with.

I slammed the door into the frame once, twice. It didn't budge. I tried it a third time before realizing that the frame was warped, and so (with strength I imagine comes from the same place as for those mothers who manage to single-handedly lift cars off of their trapped children) I braced my back leg against the wall, and with the other, pushed as hard as I could against the frame while yanking on the door. It crunched into the frame with a click, and I fell against it.

Noah was audibly relieved. I left the bathroom triumphant, meeting the eyes of everyone who glanced up in a way that said, "Yeah, what? You got something to say to me? I just got my son out of a major jam, so bring it." But I was also a little heartsore, wishing I'd have come to him earlier so that he needn't have pleaded so desperately.

He had no trouble getting out, my Noah. Just army-crawled his way under the stall door and returned to me covered in dust and gratitude.

I thought of the parable of the good Samaritan on the way home, and the simple kindnesses that mean so much, and which we neglect to show, even to the ones we are called to love first. I thought of Noah, my child in discomfort, who could not articulate what he needed, but only *that* he needed, and the gratitude on his face when he rejoined me at the table. I was privileged to show him mercy—me, his mother, who ought always to do so. I whispered a prayer into the steaming evening air on the drive home: "Please, Lord, let me always be my children's good Samaritan. No matter my own embarrassment or perceived disgrace, let them be able to always count on mercy from me.

"Oh and also, Lord, thanks for clearing the bathroom ahead of time."

~

On the day I was married, my mother doled out plenty of marital counsel. She'd have done just as well to summarize marriage thusly: "My child, there will be laundry. So much laundry." On any given week, I wash ten loads of it. More, if the sheets need to be done. More still, if Noah has led our children on the charge of "let's have an adventure!" The woods and crooked creek and deep, soft grass on the hills that undulate toward the horizon from our front door are the stuff of storybooks, and keep my children away from the electronic toys that are always threatening to seduce them. Country living is good for the soul. But it's torture on your power bill. And then, there's Noah himself, who performs more daily costume changes than Liza Minnelli at the Garden. He will eschew pajamas in favor of wearing a swimsuit to bed. Other times, he will wear underwear as a swimsuit. Sometimes, he will also wear a swimsuit to school. No one from the school has called me yet, so I'm letting it slide.

Every child with autism is different. Each of their quirks is unique. There is a saying: "If you've met one child with autism, you've met *one* child with autism." For Noah, clothing is a major issue. Of preeminent concern is comfort. Many children with ASD have sensory issues, and for some, the least obtrusive clothing label can feel like a pad of steel wool against their skin. These items of clothing are worn for brief periods of time, and then Noah "discards" them in the laundry. Or it can be that Noah decides the yellow T-shirt he put on didn't look as hip as he'd hoped. This one is tried on in the full-length closet mirror and then thrown under his bed. And despite the fact that he is a dirty-toenailed, hayloft-clambering, creek-splashing, sport-playing boy, he *absolutely refuses* to wear a pair of pj's more than once, considering the repetition somehow repugnant. I can't figure out this formula. The one time during the day that Noah wears something in which he's not actively sweating is the one outfit I can't get him to wear again. I've tried laying his pajamas back out on his bed after he gets dressed, sneaking them back into his drawer, putting them on top of his towel before he gets into the shower. Nothing works. And this doesn't count the nights when he is too hot (change of pj's rather than simply kick off the covers), or too cold (layer on every single pj he has, only to dump all of them in the laundry the next morning). If I had to estimate, I'd probably say six of the ten loads I wash each week are Noah's alone.

But with Jesse? There is no laundry that I can convince him needs doing. If given the chance, he will wear the identical outfit every day. There is a blue hooded sweatshirt that he calls his "jacket," and even if I tell him it is in the wash, he will pull it from the machine and put it on wet, comfort be hanged. There is also a flat-brimmed New York Mets ball cap, and a collared shirt underneath. The collared shirt must be layered with another (similarly collared) shirt under it. If he is forced to wear something different, the "jacket" and the cap stay, and only the shirt can be changed. In Jesse's mind, repetition is king, and "cool" trumps comfort.

I suppose I ought to count my blessings here, because only recently has Jesse given up his penchant for wearing firefighter costumes. He wore through so many costumes and their many accoutrements (belts, plastic axes, fire extinguishers), that my mother bought him three whole sets. One morning, when taking Jesse with me to Grace's eye doctor appointment, I discovered too late that Jesse was wearing two different fire boots because I'd been in too much of a hurry to oversee his dressing and had therefore relegated it to his three-year-old self. He so loved the noble profession of these civil servants that he wanted to express it with both his shoe choices, in two different colors and sizes, and so the foot that wore the larger of the two boots dragged slightly behind him in a rhythmic shuffle all day.

~

By nature, I'm a pacifist. And also, a bit of a chicken. When the time is right to be angry, my lips stay zipped. When that time is past however, I'm a veritable colossus of articulate and righteous indignation. I'm really good at getting mad after the fact.

I can't think of a single instance when my rebuttal was timely delivered, save for that one time when my staunchly left-leaning atheist of a former boss—the one who preached equality and social reform—called me a "fascist" for going to a Christian college, whereupon I managed to retort, "Oh wait. Aren't *you* the one who's supposed to be open-minded?"

Yeah. Nailed it.

But it's hard not to be angry when I ponder all the self-righteous comments and looks my boys receive when they rage in public or make improper comments or pontificate at sonic boom volume. Our burden is lots lighter than that of other parents whose children have disabilities of any sort. As high-functioning autistics, you might only notice that Noah is a little "different." That he flaps, or chews his clothing, or talks your ear off about Super Mario Brothers. You might notice that Jesse spins when he eats something he loves, or sucks his thumb when he grabs hold of my clothing, or that he cannot write his name. The verbal ability and self-sufficiency of my two Sons of Thunder often belie their uniquenesses.

From another vantage, this can make our burden seem heavy. Heavy to us only, maybe. But heavy nonetheless. Because you'd never notice their differences from a distance, you might look down your nose when, in the middle of Noah's flag football game, he halts a play to have a complete and total meltdown in the middle of the field. Or you might snort a little out of disgust when you're standing behind him in the checkout line and he remarks in full voice that the woman in front of him "sure is fat!" Remember that scene from *Terms of Endearment* when Emma doesn't have enough to pay for her groceries? Oh yes. It's just that painful. Especially when the woman in front of you turns around and sneers so hard she practically sends her lip up over her head.

So then you're faced with an onerous choice: (a) explain to the woman that you're terribly sorry, and that he isn't always able to control what he says, even though we've drilled him on appropriate responses, because he has Asperger's, you see, and lacks certain social skills and would she please forgive him; or (b) tell your son that what he said is not appropriate or nice (just like you've told him 100 previous times), and avoid eye contact with the woman altogether because you don't know if the grocery store is the most appropriate place for a discussion on his "wiring" because he has yet to be told that his autism makes him different, and this is a conversation for which you're going to need to be sitting down with your husband. And also, you like this option better because you are just too downright scared to face the woman with the acrobatic lip.

Still, something nags me: the proclamation that "There's nothing wrong with him," which we get a lot, and which makes the embarrassing parts so much harder. Because the thing that causes them is invisible, because our boys can sometimes seem so "typical," the dismissal of their disabilities happens a lot. We are, even after expert consultation that confirms their diagnoses, back to occasionally being called "reactionary." "You would never know they're on the spectrum," we hear.

But when I leave their neurology appointments at the Kennedy Krieger Institute, I always glance down at the form, like what it says is somehow going to be different from one visit to the next, as though the empty lines will no longer be filled with notes. Yet their discharge slips always tell me that they both have "static encephalopathy": an unchanging, permanent, global system of brain dysfunction. When someone questions that diagnosis, after we've worked so hard to make peace with it in the first place, it's like being told you're really in Italy when you know for a fact you're in Holland.

These are the options I've developed for how to respond to "There's nothing wrong with him" (also known as the "you're suburban alarmists with too much time on your hands and are seeing a diagnosis around every corner" syndrome):

(1) "I'm sure it seems that way, because we pay a lot of therapists a lot of money to make sure he doesn't gag at dinner when there's a candle on the table."

(2) "It may look like it, so I 'm sure you won't mind when I send him to your house the next time he has a meltdown. And would you mind teaching him to tie his shoes while he's there? Because at ten, he still doesn't know how."

Finally, this one, which is the truest, and with which I am most satisfied:

(3) "You're absolutely right. He's perfect the way God made him. With lots of dedication, prayer, and the work of exceptional specialists, his disability is less and less visible. We have worked hard to make his autism hard to see. How very fortunate and blessed we are that it is invisible to you."

When I get the statements I dislike so much, those that shoot the dart of hurt into my mother's heart, I need to take a breath and remind myself that they can't see what Noah and Jesse have, and they don't know its manifestations. They are ignorant (not in the Maury-Povich-chair-flipping "You're just bein' ignorant!" sense of the word). They literally know no better. They can't "see" our autism like we can.

That means I need to exercise a little self-control and practice the mercy I like to preach. I need to rely on that discretion at which I'm pretty adept and keep my smiling trap shut. If you're reading this and you've experienced that familiar prick of rage when someone sneers at your child who's in the middle of a public rage or who's loudly explaining to you why he thinks the person in front of him smells so bad, when you're being critiqued for the child you love so much but cannot control, here's my knowing glance, telling you that I've been there too. But be patient. They just can't see what you can.

There once was a time I thought our little man Jesse had Tourette's syndrome. I am, in my layperson's understanding of the same, hoping that the vocal tics that happen to be curse words are just part of his autism. Because I can walk by his room as he's deep in video-game play and impervious to me, and hear him chanting, "f---, f---, f---." You can imagine how this makes me feel. But the mortification is not truly complete until your five-year-old teaches his best friend—who also goes to a Christian school—what the middle finger means. Whereupon, said best friend later flips his teacher the bird and proceeds to instruct her that it is (a) a swear word, (b) *what* that swear word is, and (c) that his best friend, Jesse, taught it to him. Jesse, who is himself being raised in a Christian home. Jesse, who asks what words he can say, manipulating benign words little by little ("Yes, you may say that, Jesse") until he's gotten to a full swear word without your even noticing it ("No, you *cannot* say that, Jesse!"). There are always other people in the room when this happens, as if he wants to make sure there's an audience so everyone can fully appreciate how he's led you down the path to destruction without your even being fully aware of it.

Jesse's own teacher has suffered an earful of expletives. I swear you'd think this kid had been raised by Tarantino the way he talks. Bless her meek little heart. A few days ago, I came to retrieve Jesse along with a wave of other parents likewise scooping up their squiggly children, and I was gently nudged in the direction of a note.

"Hello there. Yes. I, um . . . well, we had an incident today, and I wanted you to read something . . ." She then pointed to a note she'd written which detailed the sequence of the day's incident, and which I'm guessing she didn't have the constitution to describe to me verbally because it contained a word none of us like to use in polite company unless we're describing what happened to Lorena Bobbitt's husband.

Yes, that word.

It read like a police log: "Jesse and Amy were playing this afternoon at 3:05 p.m. and began to fight over a toy. Jesse called Amy a 'p----' and Amy said it hurt her feelings, and then Jesse called Amy a 'p----head,' and then I made Jesse apologize to Amy and we talked about what words we should and should not use."

I would like to thank a certain unnamed spouse who refused to use euphemisms for certain body parts, believing that the actual medical terminology would better serve the early stages of our children's development. I would also like to thank my eldest son for laughing so hard the first time Jesse said it that I thought he was going to asphyxiate. And I would like to thank autism for building the neurological foundation for repetition, because any natural inclination a little boy has to laugh at or use such a word is pretty much pumped full of steroids when your child is on the spectrum. Imagine Dustin Hoffman's *Rain Man* statement "I'm an excellent driver" being replaced with "you're a p---- head," and subsequently repeated in similar fashion. Not appropriate to time, place, or audience. Ever. And it came out of my little boy's mouth—the mouth that had yet to dispatch its first baby tooth, the mouth surrounded yet by a cushion of baby fat. I have a new appreciation of the phrase "out of the mouths of babes."

And boy does it make those of us who parent such a child cringe at what he might utter next. Because the people he most listens to are us. And also, pro wrestlers. And maybe, the Discovery Health channel when I'm not looking.

~

Not long ago, I had two children in a crowded dentist's waiting room. I was eager to get their checkups complete before the start of a new school year and was already on edge. All three would be attending a new school, and I had gobs of paperwork to complete. The dentist's form was but one leaf of paper in a whole stack. I was mentally ticking off items on my to-do list as I bounced an impatient knee. I turned to Noah and Grace.

"Guys, wait right here. Mommy is going to the bathroom. It's that door, right there." I pointed to the door fifteen or so feet away.

"'K, Mom."

I came back about two minutes later, whereupon Noah stood up and loudly proclaimed to a full waiting room, "Mom! When you were in the bathroom, someone came over, sat in your seat, farted, and got up and walked away!"

Now, if I'd had less experience in, oh, say, navigating faux pas or surviving humiliation, I'd have grabbed them both by the hand and fled the office, appointment be hanged. But I am not your average mother. Chagrin is my middle name. I have loads of experience in it.

"Shhh! OK, Noah, thank you, but that's inappropriate. Let's change the subject, please."

The injury of embarrassment sometimes feels like the most pointed of any in motherhood, the most accurate in its aim, puncturing the soul's constitution that is built for protection of a little person who can't yet protect themselves. Sometimes, my children do not know what they do is embarrassing to others. Sometimes, they bring the embarrassment on themselves. In both cases, the pangs of mother empathy overcome me. It's then that I want to sweep open the arm of a magic cloak and gift them with invisibility. And me too. I want that cloak a lot. I have seen Noah ignored by his teammates when he didn't know I was looking. I have heard him talk of being picked last for school games, having his picture torn by another student in art class, or not being invited to a party—things most neurotypical children experience at some point in their lives too, but also things that I cannot help but question as related to his ASD. And when Noah speaks of these things, I suddenly feel myself small again, yearning so much for the acceptance of my peers, avoiding anything out of the ordinary at all costs. Sameness is safe. My children are many things, but camouflaged and same, they are not.

After a party last summer, our family stopped to get ice cream on the way home. I will admit this was a dubious parenting choice. It was late, they were filthy and underslept. But I made a last, mad attempt to grab the waning summer and took them anyway.

It turned out to be a hopeless parenting fail for many more reasons. Not only did the three of them manage to trash the car with sticky hands and dirty shoes while torturing each other with slaps and screams on the ride home, they also chose to play tsunami in the bathtub later that night, a venture that required three towels and a host of threats to correct. But before all that, there was the ordering of the ice cream itself.

The worker behind the glass was sweet and tolerant as I grabbed at kids running wild in the parking lot and pushed them to the counter to make their choices. Matt was distracted just then, guffawing with a moonstruck young couple sitting on the bench next to us. He is Mr. Handshake and a smile. Never met a stranger, that one. But I was negotiating a dairy disaster with three unruly children, wondering if there was anything I could possibly say to worm my way out of this, tell them ice cream at this hour would be a mistake, and maneuver them back to the car.

Right. Like it was an actual option.

The counter girl, bless her heart, was heavy set, and a dark shadow marked her chin and cheeks. A hormonal imbalance, perhaps. I internally saluted her, someone whose body, like mine, didn't always cooperate. Noah got to the window, and came face-to-face with the young woman behind the counter.

"Um . . . I want a milkshake . . . Oreo." Then he turned to me. "Mom? Why does that woman have a beard?"

In one smooth, purposeful gesture (one that may have looked like a shove, but was really just "spatial redirection"), I guided him to my left, out of the eyesight and earshot of the small glass window, and prayed she hadn't heard. Which of course was impossible, considering that he said it within eighteen inches of her forward-leaning face. Then I had the 1,000th discussion I've had with Noah about what is and what is not fitting conversation.

"Noah! That's totally inappropriate! Do you think saying something like that makes her feel good or bad? If you have a question, we can discuss it quietly in private later, but the last thing she needs is to be made to feel worse about something I'm sure already bothers her."

Ah . . . autism. It always keeps you on your toes. It is the genesis of the humiliating, irritating, and sometimes shocking. It's not just uncomfortable for the "victim," it smarts pretty hard for the mother of the "perpetrator" too.

His heart is so kind. "He means well!" I want to scream. "This isn't who he is!"

Maybe I will print calling cards. Or shall I call them "speaking" cards?

Caution. Statements made are much worse than intended.

I wish my children could leave alone the things that are better left unsaid, but mostly, impulse results in action. There is no filter. I heard someone say once that kids are for the most part trustworthy because they always tell the truth. And it is true that children are born unfiltered, but as they age, most learn what they can and cannot say. For some, what they cannot say is what they prefer to say. All the time.

But autism doesn't always make for the terrible embarrassment of your child flying naked down the hall when you have a houseful of guests, yelling that he "has to go poop" and has to do so in your bathroom "because it's the best." There are also those moments that stem from other things said. Mysterious things. Like when your son asks you for "spare parts. You know, like gears or gadgets? Because I want to build a teletransporter." Or those times when he insists that "the broccoli is too intense," or that when "Zelda kisses me, it tastes like frog! Like lily pads sunken under the water." Or when he and his sister argue language fluencies, and he baits her because he finds her brainpower inferior to his and wants to prove it:

Noah: "I speak dog and horse."

Grace: "I speak fish and eagle."

Noah: "Well, can you speak scarecrow?"

Grace: "Yes."

Noah: "Ha! Trick question. Scarecrows can't talk!"

Busted, Grace.

Even the little one surprises us with what is stored inside. Like when Jesse told us all at dinner that he wanted to add on to Noah's prayer at dinnertime. "Jesus, I sorry I broke Grace's crayons." Grace harrumphed here. Dad squeezed her knee, and Jesse continued. "And Jesus, I love Noah. He encourage me, and I encourage him."

It is then that you are awestruck by the intricacy of the thoughts in their mysterious, magnificent minds, touched by encephalopathy and perfection at the same time. For the most part, they get each other, and we get them too. Which is how we subsist when our cheeks are flushed and red. Because sometimes, when the stars align, they say exactly what we pray they will.

Which helps us do it too.

7

Fortune Favors Anyone but Me

I am not saying this because I am in need, for I have learned to be content whatever the circumstances. I know what it is to be in need, and I know what it is to have plenty. I have learned the secret of being content in any and every situation, whether well fed or hungry, whether living in plenty or in want. I can do all this through him who gives me strength.

Philippians 4:11–13

God never gives you more than you can handle, right?

I'm not so sure. Not now. Not anymore.

It's my view that some people get *more* than they can handle. Some people lie in bed laughing with that crazy-person laugh because they have lost about as much as they thought they possibly could and are still pushing forward with an unseen strength. They lose their home, their health, their jobs, their loved ones. When I think, for example, of Job—he whose wife told him to "curse God and die!" and who then went on to lose his children—I think, "Brother, how *didn't* you curse God and die?" I think of David hiding from Saul in caves near the Dead Sea, spending years as a fugitive in fear for his life, later losing his son, and crying out to a God that he loved with the whole of his heart but may have thought for a moment wasn't hearing his desperate cries.

We're never promised we won't "get more than we can handle." The closest promise we receive in this regard is 1 Corinthians 10:13, which speaks of God giving us an escape from temptations so that it's not too much to bear. But when it comes to pain, trial, heartache, woe—not once does the Bible say that we'll be spared from more than we can handle. Instead, we are admonished, "I have told you these things, so that in me you may have peace. In this world you will have trouble. But take heart! I have overcome the world" (John 16:33). Not only is our life not a rosy garden path, we are told outright to expect tribulation. The rain falls on us and on everyone else (Matt. 5:45); sometimes in a whispered sprinkle, sometimes in a downpour that soaks our beleaguered bones.

"I have learned the secret of being content in any and every situation, whether well fed or hungry, whether living in plenty or in want. I can do all this through him who gives me strength" (Phil. 4:12–13). We can do all things through Him who lifts us up and can survive the tempests that threaten to crash us against the rocks. Whether we want to survive them is a different tale altogether. It will suck at times. Believe that. And believe there will be moments that you think there is nowhere to go but into the grave to escape the pain and difficulty. There will be times that fleeing it all seems easier than dealing with it and muddling through. But getting more than we can handle forces our gaze upward for some help. If we could handle the mess on our own, we'd never have to seek God's help in managing it.

Every good sob story has to start somewhere, and everyone who's ever hurt has paused briefly or at length to shake their fist at a concealed God and express their anger as to *why He thought this was necessary*. So I'll now instruct you on how to play your own tiny violin when everything that can possibly go wrong does. To begin, take a moment to reflect on your own difficulties. Now, admit to yourself that there are probably moments in which you've acted like a raging Chihuahua and spewed out a bunch of wrathful invectives at God when things started to fall apart. This is OK. He is big enough to take it, and He will love you through it. You will probably feel foolish after it's happened and you're on your knees asking for forgiveness. I am simply speculating here (*clears throat*).

My children do a great job of illustrating this paradigm. The temper tantrum my daughter throws after she is punished for "decorating" her room with a Sharpie eventually comes to an end. My son's disappointment at being picked last for a schoolyard game will fade. I have to fight the urge to fly in and rescue them from their circumstances or their own emotions, because every challenge presents an opportunity to find a lesson. Through everything, my love for them is unchanged. The Lord is more apparent to me when my head's bowed through adversity than when my chin's held high in easy sailing. Messes make God visible.

Now I recognize God's finger poking me in the side, reminding me that I haven't been at the helm of this life. Ever. Before, when I persisted in delusions of control and perfection, when I clung to the predictability of overachievement as the barometer of value, every setback required more work. Every mistake required more diligence. My life followed an orderly, miserable formula. Now, there's very little I find predictable. Not even my own responses. Sometimes now, I am surprised at my own strength (God's strength through me) when the road ahead looks impassable, and at my own thankful spirit when part of me just wants to scream a bunch of curse words at the sky and run away because I'm afraid a lightning bolt is coming. Now, after a good pout, I usually tell Him, "OK, Lord. I'm ready. Let's go."

Some say diamonds are a girl's best friend. Me? I say diamonds are no good unless they can be sold for a profit to beat the wolves back from the door, or you can turn them back into coal so you can light a fire to keep warm. Matt thought we'd hit bottom when he had to the sell the diamond earrings he bought for me on our ten-year anniversary. They were the most valuable material thing I owned. They had represented a period of temporary prosperity—the hope of something better on the horizon—from a decade of our shared history and a period in which we admittedly knew very little about how to handle money or commit our decision making to the One who gave it to us in the first place. So as it turned out, we were headed to the trough to eat with the pigs. I was selling old electronics for grocery money, wrapping them in Tiffany

& Co. tissue paper, which, while it was the only packing material available, was also movie-script ironic. Out the door went designer handbags and home decorations, old toys and outgrown clothes. I consigned everything I could find. The earrings I sold for rent money. Rent money for a home no one would believe we were permitted to inhabit.

The house itself was a riddle: for how does a couple bet everything on a soon-to-implode real estate market, only to lose it all—every last rental property and their primary residence—and then go on to somehow find an extravagant property whose owners are looking for renters, preferably a family, and are willing to lower the rent, and don't in the least mind their animals or the fact that at least three banks have files on said couple a country mile long? How does such a sprawling residence in the bucolic countryside, with horses, barn cats, wild geese, a swimming pool, and acres of rippled hillside, make itself available to such a displaced family? Because truth is stranger than fiction, and our lives are stranger than that. This is partly due to that tendency of ours, the one toward that head-first, deep-end living. We might not test the water as often as we ought.

I think it's also due to the fact that the Lord's decided smoke signals, carrier pigeons, and billboards weren't enough to get our attention, so He pretty much had to burn everything to the ground. Then, because He saw our scraped knees, He blessed us with great things according to His great mercy.

Now I find Him when I look for Him, because He makes Himself known.

A few months after the sale of the earrings, I was wearing six layers and a ski cap around this rental home because the oil had run out. Again. In the middle of winter. During the infamous "polar vortex" of January 2014. When the temperature hit 20 below. Our house bottomed out at 51 degrees. We discovered that there was a break in the oil line between the house and the tank. If someone had been looking for oil around the house that winter, I'm sure Daniel Day-Lewis would have showed up with the cast from *No Country for Old Men* and a drilling rig. Indeed, we had been paying a local oil company every six weeks to turn the ground into a perfect fracking site. The cost of oil in this economy is incensing enough. Realizing you may have been pouring it out on your front lawn instead of burning it can send you through the blasted roof.

We ran two space heaters and set four fires in the fireplaces (yes, this is the charm of an old but poorly insulated house: lovely to look at, six fireplaces to boast of, but drafty as Swiss cheese. You could read a book by the daylight seeping in under the front door). When your body hurts a little every day, being cold is the ultimate torture because there is no place from which you can escape the joints that are tormenting you.

We are not unique in that our lives are full of tragedies and tragi-comedies. What makes us unique is perhaps the volume of them both and the speed at which they both come together: that is, at the same time without a moment to breathe, so that you think you are being pulled into some elaborate television stunt, as if yours is actually some kind of warped *Truman Show* existence. We're convinced our life would play well on the big screen.

For example, the tragi-comedy:

A span of seventy-two hours from two summers ago was both awful and funny in equal measure. Grace's beloved beta fish, Ariel, had died. I wasn't too heartbroken, as the fish had made it about one year—high achievement for something the size of a half dollar. So, we went to get another fish and decided on two tiny tiger barbs. Grace was elated. At Noah's strong suggestion, she named them "Barbara" and "Barbarian." This is the saccharine Disney moment in the story. But we are quickly headed into *National Lampoon* territory.

At the same time, Grace and Noah were approaching the last of their summer camps. This was a traditional, north-woods camp experience that we deemed their "big finish" to the summer, but which required a physical for entry. Their pediatrician couldn't get them in until September. Had I waited too long to make the appointments? Yes. Yes, I had. So we took them to the Target "Minute Clinic" for a checkup and a signature on the all-important health documentation. We did this on a Saturday. Two weeks before the start of school. On a Saturday. After gymnastics and karate classes. Before Jesse's nap. On a *Saturday*.

Two hours, three screaming children, and two signatures later, Matt was headed home with the kids in my car, and I was headed home with a trunk full of groceries in his. A party followed that night, wherein Jesse peed himself and spent the rest of the evening undressed from the waist down. I'd apparently gotten lax in potty training the third time around, because while it wasn't the first of our training mishaps, I'd yet to stick a spare pair of undies and shorts in the car. Apparently, I thought I was too good for a backup plan.

That evening, I reviewed a copy of the MRI report sent to me by my doctor after my recent brain scan. You see, I have Behcet's disease, a form of autoimmune vasculitis that can attack any portion of the 62,000 miles of blood vessels in the body, which means my disease is like a box of chocolates. You never know what . . . well, you know how it goes. After some disconcerting neurological symptoms (including memory loss and problems of cognition), I underwent an MRI that revealed subtle changes in the white matter of my brain, probably due to cerebral vasculitis (up to 20 percent of patients like me suffer from a subset of the disease involving the brain). Not knowing when to leave well enough alone, I hit the internet. What came up was *vascular dementia*. I turned to Matt.

"Well, it's official. I've finally lost my mind."

We thought we would sleep in on Sunday and give everyone a chance to recover from the previous day and get ready for a busy week. Our adorable and hatefully energetic Zelda had other plans, and decided she would set to work destroying not only an entire wall of basement insulation, but part of the heirloom crib that's been in Matt's family three generations. We had begun the postapocalyptic cleanup job before we realized that the shop vacuum was missing its filter. Matt headed to Home Depot, and I resettled my overstimulated, underslept three-year-old in his bed for a nap no fewer than four times before we began repairing in earnest. Jesse repaid my patience by knocking down the hall table and sending a filled vase careening down the second-floor landing. "I forgive you!" he yelled at me, clearly not understanding the concept. *"I forgive you!"* He was desperate, and heart-wrenchingly reminded me, "I a good kid, Mama! I a hero," which is what your preschooler says to you when you have said something you regret (or screamed it, perhaps) in the midst of a reprimand.

With the basement finally in order, we sat down to dinner. I filled Noah's plate. Noah's eyes filled with water. He stifled a gag, insisting, "There's gasoline in these Brussels sprouts!" I fought the urge to retort, "So eat them anyway, and make sure not to light a match." Sunday night, Matt and I collapsed into bed, making it until 4:00 a.m., when Jesse got up and insisted, "It's mornin' time!"

Monday morning, the kids were scheduled to be at camp by 8:45 a.m. In a flurry, I sent Matt down to our neighbor's house so he could feed their dogs and let them out. Our friends were taking a well-deserved trip to the beach, and we had agreed to dog sit. Matt was back within a few minutes and pulled me aside.

"Prince is dead."

I don't know what I looked like at that point, but I'm pretty sure I made whatever face cartoonists draw to indicate surprise. I think there was an exclamation point above my head.

For you dog lovers, let me say that Prince was thirteen (that's ninety-one in people years if you're doing the math), on heart medication, and of very limited mobility. There was no indication of pain or suffering in his passing, and Matt was there to be with him at the end. It was definitely Prince's time to go. But I wasn't thinking about that when Matt came home. All I could think of was how to pull off a three-ring circus in ninety minutes.

Matt and I powwowed quickly, and decided to get Grace and Noah to camp, drop Jesse off with the neighbor's nanny, go back to the house to tend to our neighbor's other dog, and load their deceased dog in the back of Matt's car so I could take it to the vet and Matt could be ready for his 10:00 a.m.

conference call. All this, I was going to attempt with a husband who had (1) a rotator cuff tear and (2) compound fractures from a recent shoulder dislocation. He literally could not lift his fork without moaning.

Somewhere between the mania of heartache and humor, as we were loading Prince into our car, I looked at my husband and blurted, "There's no one I'd rather carry a dead dog with than you!" Because it's true. Because I love him the way only God can show you how to love another person—through all the mess and because of it.

God was in an open pet shop and the smile on Grace's face when she gingerly held her bag of new fish on the way home. God was in the signatures on the medical forms that got Noah and Grace into, as Noah called it, "Camp I-Wanna-Pee-Pee." God was in an excuse to redecorate (cheaply, natch) because a vase was broken and in Zelda's wagging tail and cocked head—so excited to see us. So very covered with insulation. And God was in Matt's rescheduled meeting that meant he was with me that Monday morning and able to help, instead of in North Carolina as originally planned.

"He lifted me out of the slimy pit, out of the mud and mire; he set my feet on a rock and gave me a firm place to stand" (Ps. 40:2). Thank You, Lord, for a firm place to stand. Thank You for reaching out Your hand to me when I'm covered in mire, because You love me, even when I'm a mess. Thank You for loving all of us both now, and when we were drawing straws to see who would flush Barbara down the toilet.

Then, there come the tragedies.

The hospital is always a good place to start because beginning a sentence with "So-and-so is sick with x-y-z and is in the hospital," I have learned, is a good way to get everyone at a party to shut up at the same time. There is something about a hospital that forces our gaze toward the heavens and shoves in our faces the remembrance that we're lucky to even have one more day. There are chapels and atriums lofty and airy, driving skyward in a cathedral of glass and steel, and anxious faces, tapping fingers, pacing feet. Perhaps it's the recognition of the fragility of our bodies that reminds us of how we are greater than our mechanical parts, but not their Author. It could be that we are forced to reckon with our loss of control as we're hooked to a monitor, or waiting for a loved one's safe return from surgery. The failing of our bodies, these cracked and fragile jars in which we hold our treasure, remind us that we need Someone bigger than us to fix our broken pieces.

"Please," we breathe into clasped hands. "Please, let it be OK."

After Jesse's birth and before the brain MRI that elucidated more versions of my body's weirdness, I had become sick with something that didn't have a name. I was running fevers, woke in the night with soaking sweats, found my skin changing for the worse. I spent two years searching for a medical diagnosis that evaded us. It wasn't uncommon to see two or three doctors in a single week. We visited specialists all over the state, and it was hinted by some that it might just be "middle-class wife syndrome." It was very hard not to ask these doctors if they'd heard of "supercilious jerk" syndrome.

I was in daily pain. I was begging the Lord for answers. My husband stood by my side. He never faltered. At some point, I stopped asking for answers and started asking for contentment. "Give me strength for the day," I prayed. "Let me be the best parent and wife I can be." I reasoned that if the Lord wasn't going to tell me what this thing was that I had, I needed to come to peace with how to deal with it. After I ended up in the hospital with meningitis, body-wide ulcers, and swollen joints, I finally received my diagnosis of Behcet's disease through the National Institutes of Health in the spring of 2011. Behcet's is a form of autoinflammatory vasculitis so rare that only 15,000 in the US are speculated to have it. The world expert on the condition flies in to the center in New York to see patients from every continent. I am on a fistful of daily medications that keeps my broken-down body on the level. For now.

Yes, only I would have something so weird and rare and hard to pronounce. Only I would require a world expert for treatment.

Typical.

A few months later, Matt, my father, and I flew back to my home state of Wisconsin for my grandmother's memorial service. My brother Sam and his wife Allison flew out from California to meet us. Sam looked flushed. He complained of being tired, that something was "off," and he was having trouble pinpointing it. I told him to check with his doctors and suggested some causes. Understanding the frustration of medical ambiguity, I tried to encourage him to be aggressive.

I suppose one could call this tactic "successful," because Sam's aggression in seeking answers to his own unknown illness resulted in a diagnosis of Hodgkin's lymphoma. The context of this diagnosis is astonishing and also falls in the "only *your* family, Sarah" category: Sam's diagnosis came two decades after my mother's mother and both her brothers had been diagnosed with blood-borne cancers of their own. All three of them had hit the genetic jackpot within nine months. I think again of the radium in Waukesha's water, because I cannot speculate any other reason for the sideshow version of our family's medical mysteries. The eventual determination of Sam's similar cancer caused gaping mouths everywhere we went. He started chemotherapy within two months. The prognosis was good. We were wounded, but hopeful.

The next year, in 2012, my husband's ebullience at the beach during a July 4th vacation nearly cost him his shoulder. Two fractures, one bone chip, two torn tendons, and a dislocation later, I was sitting at the cafeteria in Union Memorial hospital in Baltimore, shaking my head over how such a benign incident (jumping into a wave on the last day of vacation) could become so very complex. After surgery, I knew Matt would be in an immobilizer for six weeks and would need someone else to do almost everything for him. Then, he would begin a grueling physical therapy regime that, if we were lucky, would return him to pre-accident status in about six months to a year. All because he jumped in the ocean on vacation.

Matt spent a lot of time being angry after the accident. No one would begrudge him that. (In truth, "angry" might be too kind a distinction. "Raging," "stiff-necked," "irrational," and "vitriolic" would all serve similarly here.) Why would God permit a family vacation to end in such a catastrophic way? Why couldn't the water have been deeper, the wave higher?

Why a dislocation and all the associated injuries? Matt's shoulder injury was just one more thing on an already long litany of crises to deal with. We were over it. I was over the moaning and whining too. Matt and I had been playing the "who hurts more" game, and we were sick of it.

But who were we to be mad? Did we profess to know better than God did as to what purpose this ridiculous health detour served any of us? I thought of what Job reminded his wife when she snarled that he ought to just curse God and die: "'You are talking like a foolish woman. Shall we accept good from God, and not trouble?' In all this, Job did not sin in what he said" (Job 2:10). Were Matt and I going to accept good from Him, and not trouble? Did we really think our married life was going to be a cinch?

"Don't be impressed with your own wisdom. Instead, fear the LORD and turn away from evil. Then you will have healing for your body and strength for your bones" (Prov. 3:7–8 NLT).

Matt and I were both desperate for healing. Our bodies and souls were broken and weary. God showed me that our frustration was just an expression of our own wisdom. We learned that one cannot hold trust and frustration, both. By trusting God, giving Him our hearts, accepting His plan and moving on, the pride was cleared from our eyes, and we were shown what really mattered.

What really mattered was not how many doctors we had to see before finding the one that gave a rat's you-know-what about our conditions. What mattered was what I said to my husband in the waiting room, and how his hand felt in mine as we prayed together for the surgeon's steady hand and a safe return from anesthesia. What really mattered wasn't the circus I needed to coordinate to get the kids to school and still make it to the hospital by 6:00 a.m., but the bleary-eyed face that greeted me from under a blue hospital bonnet, and an eventual grin that shows up from underneath my husband's freckles. What mattered wasn't how much we hurt, but Who we could turn to for healing. Because He loved us, and was faithful. No matter how much we complained.

One day, in the lobby of a Quest Diagnostics in the summer of 2013, I buried my nose in Noah's hair. Grace's hair is as fine as her mother's and just as challenging to style. She recently requested a blunt bob which is just one pouncing kitty short of YouTube cute. Jesse's is fine too, but even when clean, I can run my hands through it and get it to stand straight up. Its gritty coarseness could be its natural texture or the pomade of little-boy dirt I can never quite get out.

Noah's hair, though, is thick and wiry, like the coat of a beaver. It is the kind of hair that will one day usher him into the ranks of the hair elite, those for whom male pattern baldness is unknown territory. My father has this kind of hair. His is salt-and-pepper, sea-captain thick with a natural wave that he manages to make all the more awesome by the occasional running of his fingers through it. Though he is oblivious, other men quietly detest him for this hair. This is understandable. At sixty-four, we shouldn't have hair growing long enough to tie into a ponytail. It shouldn't be curling out under the brim of his ball cap in perfect, grayish waves. It should be lying flat and frail under the weight of a wet comb-over, shellacked with drugstore gel, or shaved off entirely to spare the wearer the indignity of trying to fake a head of hair when everyone knows he's pretty much bald. He has better hair than just about any woman I've seen. It's disgusting, really.

As required by the blood draw guidelines, Noah had gone some fourteen hours without eating, but that wasn't the only thing making him woozy. Our neurologist, after reviewing our storied family health history, decided that genetic testing might prove beneficial. He'd barely gotten out the words before I was calling the lab to make an appointment, offering my son up like some sacrificial lab rat. It seemed the thing to do. Our family chromosomes are so dirty, they should come with an NC-17 rating.

The first lab had expired tubes—ones that were needed for some of the more exotic blood work. We headed to the next. The waiting room was overrun. We weren't called for some time, and then after an hour, when a room finally opened, Noah was sitting in the draw chair shaking like a leaf, the hands pressed up against his closed eyes were a mottled purple. Because, after all, this is exactly what a kid with autism needs: to be told he's going to get a needle and then to draw out the wait for as *long* as possible. I bent down to kiss his head and breathed deep of the dusty, "stuffed animal" smell his hair emits, that combination of little boy, French fry, sweaty clothes, and mischief that I just adore. When I looked up, I saw a man of a certain age pass by, pompadour of hair coated in an unnatural, toneless black and sprayed into obedience. Behind him shuffled a wisp of a woman with a sweater around her shoulders, though the temperature outside was well into the 80s. Her face was taut with the burden of steroids, but the rest of her was fragile and spindly as porcelain. Her hair was as toneless as her husband's and seemed unsteady on her head. I realized then it was a wig and wondered for what cancer she'd been undergoing chemo. This would have been one of those "routine" blood draws to determine how much more toxicity her body could bear in an effort to destroy an unseen enemy. I wondered how much time she'd been told she had. Two hours in a lab no longer seemed interminable.

I looked down at Noah, who was bouncing his knees, asking me if I could pinch his arm and show him what the needle was going to feel like so he could be prepared. I thought of the metabolic disorders Dr. Rubenstein was digging for: diabetes, hemochromatosis, Wilson's disease. I prayed silently that nothing would show up in his blood work. Then I gently pinched a little fold of skin in the crook of Noah's arm. His eyes lit up. "That's it?"

"Yep, pretty much. Do you want me to dance the Charleston?" I crossed my eyes at him, and he laughed.

What matters is what God really gives you when He gives you an illness or a disability, whether it's Behcet's disease, or lymphoma, autism, or ADHD. What comes with all the handy codes is the dose of patience, that modicum of insight, some gratitude, more kindness, or the perseverance to get up and face the day when you'd rather make a tent out of your bed sheets and permanently move inside it. This is what in His great wisdom God gives us to go along with the "awful" thing we'd rather do without, the ineffable qualities that come from facing hardship head-on and laughing while you crush its head under your heel. Because my own portion now includes dealing with an illness of my own, because I know what it is to hurt, I can better put myself in Noah's position and love him more completely. And when he feels as if his skin has been turned inside out, when sensations, fabrics, tastes, or motions are too much for him as they often are for autistic children, his screams no longer frighten me, for they are often my own heart's cry: "My flesh and my heart may fail, but God is the strength of my heart and my portion forever" (Ps. 73:26).

Before Noah knew it, nine vials of blood, a phone call to the hospital, and a few numbers confirmed in a resource book later, it was over. I walked out into the pouring rain and put my arm around Noah, who held out his bandaged arm like a purple heart. I thanked God for the things that don't matter and can be overcome, and for the things that do and train our spirits toward gratitude and strength. I thanked Him for contentment in everything, which I'm not yet fantastic at, but am striving for, every day. I stuck my nose in Noah's thick hair again, and thanked God for our hairy days.

We learned later that all the tests were negative, so in this part of our disheveled life, God injected a little bit of order, and with it, a lot of His oft-sought peace.

~

In February of 2014, a second ice storm blew in after the polar vortex of a few weeks prior. We found ourselves once again without heat, though this time we couldn't blame an empty oil tank. Instead, we—like the other 76,000 Marylanders west and north of us—were powerless for three days. In a rural area on well water, no power means no showers, no hand washing, no toilet flushing, no lights, and definitely no heat. Our place stank like a port-o-pot at the state fair, and every extremity was numb. The generator we had was enough to run two space heaters, the refrigerator, and enough electronics to keep the little ones occupied. We filled water jugs at a friend's house and used them to fill toilet tanks for flushing. I sent my children to school on the third day (their first day back after yet another days-long weather-related hiatus), and Jesse cried as he pushed his head through a heavy sweater, complaining of the cold and his aching legs. My heart burned for my children because of their discomfort, but I thought, "Soon enough, this will pass. They will be at school, where it is warm, and where the toilets are flushable, and where their lunch will be hot. And maybe if we're lucky, the power will be back on when they get home. Soon enough, it will get better."

I did not know that soon enough, it would get worse.

I was sitting next to a napping Matt in our bedroom, under four blankets, with Zelda between us, watching the space heater rotate, and waiting for literary inspiration. I surfed the news and looked outside at the glittering landscape and the squirrels on unsteady footing. I had a strange, surreal moment of prescient peace. I smiled out the window at nothing in particular, and at everything in our lives. How funny and strange and wonderful this journey of ours was. How vast the things we'd seen and survived and learned.

The phone rang. I set it to ignore, not wanting to wake Matt. Then a text showed up from my mom: "Sarah—it's urgent that you call us right away." Yikes, I thought. I left the room and dialed her number. Dad answered.

"Sarah, we were on the way to North Carolina. Is Matt there?"

"Yea, but he's napping. This 54-degree house wasn't helping us with REM sleep last night," I joked.

"I need you to wake him up, honey."

A softball of anxiety started to mount in my chest.

"Oh, OK." I sprinted down the hall in my socks, nearly upending myself on the hardwood floor. I shook Matt awake.

"It's Mom and Dad. They said it's urgent."

He sat up, and I put Dad on speakerphone. The phone lay between us like a deck of cards, small, unobtrusive. It was quiet on the other end of the line. Then Dad began:

"I got a call from Ally this morning. She had let Sam sleep in the bed, while she slept on the couch. He needed the rest." My brother Sam, the one who had survived bacterial meningitis, and an accidental gunshot to the head, and lymphoma. My brother, who had undergone chemotherapy and developed an accompanying set of symptoms that caused excruciating head pain. My brother Sam who was always sick, but always recovered. My brother who had just called me a few days ago, wishing me a happy birthday, and reminding me I was older than him, joking I was just "old" in general.

"Sarah, I'm so glad you were born," Sam had said, just a few days before.

My dad went on. "Ally went in to check on him this morning. And honey . . ."

My dad, always articulate, paused here. There was a catch that interrupted his cadence. I knew he was struggling to say something that was going to change everything, for all time.

"Your brother's gone."

"No!" I yelled into the phone. "*No, no, no!* You're *wrong!* You're *wrong!*" I began shaking.

"I'm so sorry, honey."

I don't remember the rest of the conversation. I had fled to the bathroom and fallen facedown on the floor, sobbing. Matt finished a conversation with Dad somehow, and then came over and wrapped his arms around my prone body.

"Baby, it's OK. I'm here. I'm so very sorry. I'm so sorry."

I curled myself into a ball, crying that ugly cry where everything in your face is leaking. At that moment, I very much hated God for what seemed the incomprehensible decision to take a thirty-six-year-old man away from his wife and three young daughters. This, to me, was the ultimate severance from the Lord whom I had loved and followed my whole life. Matt and I had weathered difficulty—even thrived in its wake—and yet I had still fallen from a cliff I hadn't foreseen. Like everyone who has ever lost someone, and particularly those for whom the loss is so sudden, I was plagued with "whys." I felt very much like everyone else in the world who has raised their fists at heaven in a fury of earthly misunderstanding and finite knowledge. I knew there was loss all around me; silent struggles of those for whom the surface of life belies an undercurrent of hardship. I was struck by my sameness with them, and yet the feeling that there could not be anyone in the world who possibly hurt this much.

Except for your mother, the Lord whispered. *Except for your mother who buried a brother at thirty-nine and will now bury a son at thirty-six.*

Matt pulled me off the floor and into his arms. "I am here. We will get through this together. I promise."

In the following forty-eight hours, we managed to book five airline tickets, a rental car, and six nights in a California hotel with my parents and youngest brother. We crafted care instructions for our kids and our animals, wrote medical releases in case something should happen, notified their teachers, packed for a week, and stocked the house with groceries. I will look back on this brief period and then wonder how it was all done so quickly and correctly, as if it can be said there is a "right" way to course-correct an entire family in the onslaught of grief. And then I will remember that it was God. Other explanations evade me.

The funeral ceremony came together in similar perfection, with an availability of musicians and a pastor and a chapel that wouldn't have made sense to anyone else but those who knew the Lord was behind it all, even the tragedy that no one could explain. My parents were insistent that the gospel be preached above all. Because, as my mother said, "This is the definition of why Christ went to the cross! So that death" (pointing to my brother laid out in the funeral home) "would not get the last word!"

There, in my brother's prone body, lay the gospel message itself, with all its messiness and hope and ultimate, universal order. There lay the only thing to which any of us can ever truly cling, stemming from the chaos of what seemed the worst thing imaginable. That pain of ours, it was all for something.

All those who spoke about him remarked on Sam's unwavering faith and his commitment to the belief that God was both the author of all things and the only possibility for their success. A number of co-workers of Sam's were in attendance that day, some of whom were atheists, some of whom had ribbed Sam for his stalwart Christianity. On the day of his funeral, they were exposed to the very gospel message itself.

Who can know why the Lord blesses some, and stays His hand from blessing others; why He permits hardship for the one, and ease for the other. What do I have? Blessings and hardship both, knit tightly, flowing side by side, some so close that they succeed one another in a single day. I have learned, as Paul wrote, to be content in all things: in plenty and in want, because my earthly portion includes both.

William Henry Channing, a nineteenth-century clergyman, summed up his philosophy of life like this: "To live content with small means; to see elegance rather than luxury, and refinement rather than fashion; to be worthy, not respectable; and wealthy, not rich; to listen to stars and birds, babes and sages, with open heart; to study hard; to think quietly, act frankly, talk gently, await occasions, hurry never; in a word, to let the spiritual, unbidden and unconscious, grow up through the common."[1] I aspire to live this way. I seek to do justice, love kindness, and walk humbly with God (Micah 6:8). I yearn for the contentment that only comes from stripping away the things that once seemed to matter most: money, health, houses. Even a brother.

Amid the chaos of our lives, what does God know? According to Jesse, "He knows how expensive houses are." Even here, I can only take Jesse's innocent speculation as a reinforcement of previous, difficult lessons on money management and real estate investing. Without his knowing, Jesse reminds us of the necessity to open our hands to everything. And to maybe look before we leap.

My family and I, our portions include burdens and comforts, tragedies and tragi-comedies, failing flesh, but the power of God. We have plenty of one to deal with the other, and a growing contentment in all things. We have lost much, failed grandly, hurt often. But we are newly content.

These cracked jars of ours, they overflow.

8

Leaning Towers and Other Structural Improbabilities

From him the whole body, joined and held together by every supporting ligament, grows and builds itself up in love, as each part does its work.

Ephesians 4:16

When Noah and Jesse were first diagnosed, I went around sulking like I wore a name tag: "Hi, my boys have autism." Of course, they had more than just that. But additional diagnoses, like oppositional defiance disorder, for example, just come across as "O.D.D." Which I suppose in some respects would have felt more accurate to me then, because I did feel odd and distinct from the rest of the world, sorry for both myself and for them. Particularly so in the early stages with Noah, because he was the first. Here was something that (though it's as prevalent as 1 in 88 children) made Matt and me feel very much alone. We went from feeling "normal" to feeling "abnormal."

I remember Matt, Noah, and me going to get lunch after Noah's diagnosis. We were leaving Kennedy Krieger, which is one of the foremost autism centers in the world. There's where we would later be fortunate enough (on very short notice and against the odds, as the wait list is legend) to also have Jesse evaluated. But on this day, our journey with autism had just begun. And Matt and I were shell-shocked, staring at each other in the parking lot of the clinic. Finally one of us asked if anyone was hungry. Noah was. Noah is always hungry. But not for rice. Never for rice. Because to Noah, rice, like certain other things, tastes like sand. Or dirt. Or a combination of the two. Then, if you tell him you're joking and rice isn't on the menu after all, he will sigh with relief and tell you, "You're just picking at my boots" or "squeezing my belly," which is autism-speak (to wit, a creation of Noah's mind and his alone) for "messing around with me."

Noah insisted on eating somewhere that had chicken wings. He is a boy of vast contradiction and intense preference. Noah eats chicken wings like he is solely responsible for making a dent in their worldwide numbers. I'm sure poultry from Tuscaloosa to Taiwan is begging for clemency to avoid the rabid, little-boy mouth that can never get enough of their chicken flippers. And the hotter they are, the better. He bet me once he could eat a ghost pepper. The closest he came was the "blazin'" wing at Buffalo Wild Wings. Despite his sweating brow and crimson lips, he claimed he loved them. The two glasses of water he drained told us otherwise. I'm sure you've already guessed he gets this ineluctable stubbornness from his father (who, on a related note, is also a connoisseur of wings and spicy food. And also, obstinacy). Wings are always a source of contradiction for Noah, because though he loves them, he cannot stand the mess they make and stops between each wing to wipe his fingers and face completely. They are a labor of love that persists to this day, and which requires about two hours for maximum enjoyment.

On the day of his diagnosis, I remember looking at him with his mouth ringed in an orange-red circle of sauce, thinking that everything was going to change, and we were on the path to a lifetime of hardship. Then, I remember the twenty minutes after lunch that Noah spent disrobing in the restaurant bathroom, as this too is a labor of love (and length).

When the Behcet's diagnosis and the real estate foreclosures and Jesse's diagnosis all followed in quick succession, I felt further separated. My challenges made me unique. Looking back, I realize that I was on some self-prescribed mission of solitary strength. I did not ask for help and, accordingly, did not get any. No one knows how to support you if you never tell them how.

Fine, I thought. I'm just going to take all my hardships and go mope in the corner.

Then my best friend Michelle went in for a routine mammogram. After the procedure, and while she was still in the examining room, the nurse told her to "wait here, I'm going to get the doctor." I can only imagine the tiny fireworks of fear that were igniting in her head. I had been in that place once too; that place of alpine-level oxygen deprivation, when someone with a white coat tells you after a procedure that you should "wait right there." There has to be a better way to communicate the unspoken message of "I'm about to tell you something scary, so brace yourself." Like, sending in a manicurist, or turning on *Bridget Jones's Diary* before someone slips you the bad news.

I sent Michelle a text message later that day: "How did it go?"

The very nonchalant style in which she answered—typical of her steel-chinned response to whatever may be falling down around her—made me have to pick up my phone and read the message twice to make sure I'd comprehended what she'd said:

"They found some cancer."

Some cancer? I turned to Matt.

"She said 'some' cancer! What is she talking about? That's like being a 'little bit' pregnant! It's either a yes or a no! I think Michelle just told me she has cancer!"

Inasmuch as someone can "yell" through a text message, I responded,

"What do you mean?"

She came back: "It's invasive ductal carcinoma."

I was typing a response but my hands were shaking, and so it took me an infuriating three minutes to get out, "Where are you right now?"

"At the house."

"I'm coming to see you! Don't move!"

When Matt and I found Michelle at her house, it was a week into the New Year, and Christmas decorations still adorned her fresh fir tree and the fireplace mantel. The fir was a tree she had picked out with her sons and husband, and which she had planned on planting soon to mark the Christmas she had spent with her family in that home. I wondered if she had looked at the tree and thought for a moment long or short whether it was the last Christmas tree she would decorate with her two young boys.

When we arrived, Michelle greeted us with a smile and a hug. I was dumbfounded at her strength of presence. Of the two of us, I was the one crying. I told her how sorry I was. I was particularly sorry that she was holding it together better than I was.

"I'm a fighter," she pronounced. "God's gonna take care of me. I'm going to be just fine." If she was terrified, she didn't show it. *That*, I thought, is real strength in the face of difficulty.

She did not believe the Lord had abandoned her just because her path had become rocky. And if she did at any point, I didn't know it. What I saw from her was faith and more faith, and more faith, still.

Matt and I put our hands on her shoulders and prayed for her as earnestly as we've ever prayed for anything. We wept and hugged her, and when the time came for her surgery, I cleared everything from the day and went to the hospital. Her husband met me in the waiting room.

"How is she? How did it go?"

"It went well." He gave me a wan smile. "She's out now. You can go see her if you'd like."

I found Michelle's bed from an aisle of identical rooms in recovery, and slipped in beside her. Her eyes were closed. I pulled her hand up and into mine. She smiled first, then she opened her eyes.

"How are you feeling?" I brushed the hair back from her head with my free hand.

"Good. The doctor says he got it all, plus a good margin for safety. It was easy." Yes. She would be the only person I ever knew who could call cancer surgery "easy."

She looked up at me through half-closed lids. "You look like an angel."

I chuckled, thinking the morphine drip must have felt pretty good right about then. "Why, thank you."

"Really. I know God sent you to my bedside to bless me. You came to see me. That means so much." A smile crawled across her semiconscious face.

She patted my hand. I felt my spirit lighten. I had blessed her. What a gift to care for someone in such a way that they call you an angel.

The year after, a year after medications and multiple radiation treatments, I would be sitting with Michelle on my couch, tearfully praying for her mother who was about to undergo quintuple bypass surgery. We would also be praying for my brother Sam who was then lying in a hospital bed with a staph infection on the other side of the country. I was learning that things like a $1,200 vet bill we'd just been handed for our elderly dog's ruptured tendon were really small bananas. (Note: Matt asked how healthy Jackson was, and if really, it was just better to "let him go." To which the vet responded, "Uh, he's in perfect health. I cannot euthanize a perfectly healthy dog." Drat!)

When your challenges seem small in comparison to someone else's, the Lord sure does make it easy to help shoulder another person's burdens for a while. I have found that from whatever quantity of difficulty you have, and from a seemingly random interaction with friend or stranger, will always spring the further abundance of a soul whose strength has not yet been tapped. Here, in my life, the act of comparison—that source of quiet soul angst upon which I once sketched a picture of my worth because I never felt I matched up—proved an unexpected blessing. Nothing I dealt with ever seemed as awful as that with which someone else was saddled. The Lord saw fit to ensure that.

It was a funny way to praise God, but a way nonetheless.

My husband and I are possessed of intensely competitive spirits. There is no casual game of Scrabble for us. We have been known to go silent with one another after an aggressive game of Trivial Pursuit. *Jeopardy* sounds great after dinner, but it sets the loser sulking afterward. OK really, the only person who sulks is me. The kids know better than to interrupt us when it's on. I am perched on the edge of the couch, biting my cuticle in anticipation of the next question. My husband reclines in the corner of the couch with nary a nervous manifestation.

Huh. I just realized this is the consummate picture of our marriage.

This drive to win has its benefits, of course. But I've recognized its rather tricky manifestations in Noah, who exhibits a competitive spirit differently than the average ten-year-old might. I wish none of us wanted to win as badly as we Perrys do. It's a real pain in the tail when someone's always having to be pulled out of the doldrums of a second-place finish.

Matt and I are of a mind that all kids excel at something, and it is a parent's job to encourage a child's interests so it can be discovered where that excellence lies. Our kids are excellent talkers, that much is clear. And it's required no encouragement whatsoever. But Grace, Noah, and Jesse have also shown an interest in a bunch of other things, so somewhere in our house are five karate belts, two football trophies, three swimming certificates, and a closetful of outgrown cleats. There is also a recorder with some sheet music, a tiny soccer uniform, and a purple gymnastics leotard that at some point was converted to a swimming suit. Noah recently begged to play lacrosse, which, considering the size of the ball and the hand-eye coordination required, may as well for Noah be called "catch the grape with the toothpick." Grace has recently professed her undying passion for horses, and riding lessons have ensued. Matt keeps giving me the stink eye because my dragging Grace to the barn with me gave her the idea in the first place. So now we're financially hosed.

At Noah's own urging, we have ushered him into many an athletic endeavor: wrestling, soccer, football. We never pressed, but after Noah's interest in something was piqued, we were eager to encourage it. Our thinking was twofold: (1) nurture any interest he shows in group activities, and (2) get him involved in group activities. Because kids with ASD love their solitary worlds, he might otherwise have been content to sit at home all day and play video games. But as is also common with kids on the spectrum, Noah struggles with physical endeavors. The kid has the muscle tone of Gumby, and he's about four inches wide when you look at him sideways. It wasn't until the age of eight that he learned to ride a bike. He runs like a pre-oiled Tin Man in *The Wizard of Oz*. But sweet cream cheese, he's determined. When he sets his mind to something, he's already chugging down the tracks before you tell him yes. And because Noah lacks the gross motor ability of his teammates, this is particularly challenging. More often than not, he will miss a goal or drop a pass. He doesn't understand why effort is not always commensurate with success. He is never satisfied with anything other than a win, and brings home more tears than trophies. After a game, Noah will wipe his eyes with that desperate, repetitive motion, trying to hide the fact that he's crying, and all he succeeds in doing is making his face redder until I'm screaming inside, "Make the pain stop!" Though no matter what I say, I can't seem to take his pain away, which, if you're a parent of any decency, feels like someone's knifed you in the gut.

On this note, not even the doctor is permitted to see Noah cry when we're at his office. It doesn't matter if it's strep throat or a shattered femur. Restaurant bathrooms are a good getaway, for there, he crouches under the downward tilt of the automatic dryer and lets the hot rush of air evaporate his tears. A boy of many contradictions, Noah is agog at the prospect of public embarrassment, but will wear a pair of slip-on cargo pants in his little brother's size because having to button or zip drives him batty. Sure. Because no one's going to notice a ten-year-old boy in size 5 pants.

As a way to spend more time together and encourage Noah's athletic pursuits, Matt took on a coaching position with a boys' recreational football team last year. For a kid whose brain already functions with particular deficits, I wasn't real keen on Noah donning a helmet and taking it on the chin (or in the ear, or in the back). But I've since learned that there is nothing like running a set of sideline-to-sideline gassers to wear out a kid who has pent-up energy. He sleeps better, he eats more, he is generally easier to be around. And so far, my anxieties about injuries have proved unfounded: Noah hates the concept of getting hit so much that he's developed a spin-and-run technique which eliminates the possibility of any contact whatsoever. He can't catch well, and he rarely makes a tackle, but the boy can run. Dad also helped by slotting Noah in the center position. During football season, all he has to do is snap and get out of the way. Brilliant.

Matt is the Pied Piper of little athletes. For reasons not fully known to me, they swarm to his big frame, bigger voice, and intense style of instruction like he's Mickey at Disney. I practically have to claw them off of him after practices. What I have noticed, however, is the consistency of his behavior and the steadiness of his love. This, I think, is what brings them back. He is a "supporting ligament" in the body of Christ. Matt is a connector, and nowhere is this more evident than in his coaching.

Every practice starts the same, with the same fundamentals, the same drills. Each boy knows what to expect. From there, they move into "football-y" things (I don't know the technical term for what happens next, but it all looks like it makes sense to those kids. It's also a source of certain embarrassment that I don't know what these "football-y" things are, as my lineage includes an All-American football player, as well as a Steelers draft pick, and a grandfather who received a coaching offer from the Denver Broncos. If you ask me to name a play, I will probably pretend I'm choking on a nacho so I can leave the room).

At the end of every practice, each boy gets a hug and an "I love you." Matt is a tactile guy. The extent to which this manner of leadership freaks some parents out is always evident in the grown-up faces at the first few practices. But as a youth pastor once told us, "Every kid needs a grown-up other than their parents to be wild about them." And Matt is. It's what makes these grade school kids play their hearts out on the field. But it's also what makes them hurt so bad when they lose. No one wants to disappoint their biggest fan.

This moral played out in small form, with small helmets, on a shortened field, in tiny bleachers when Matt and the Jarrettsville Ravens reached the play-off game. Noah, Matt, two other coaches, and fourteen kids were up against the Bel Air Terrapins. So great was the money in the Terrapins football program that they had their own mini-stadium with a turf field, complete with concession stand and announcer's tower. Our kids had been playing on regular old grass, next to a busted-up equipment shed, and we had to bring folding chairs or sit on our backsides in the dirt to watch a game. The snapper was autistic, the defensive tackle was a juvenile diabetic, an offensive "lineman" was actually a girl, and one of our best athletes was prone to bawling his eyes out when he made a mistake on the field. So if you're thinking this sounds very much like the "Bad News Bears," you'd be right.

Which is why, when the play-offs loomed and the boys were exuberant with the possibility of a victory, there wasn't a family member among them who'd not eaten their nails to the quick. The Ravens were the number four seed, and the

Terrapins were the number one. The first time they had played each other, the Terps had beat the Ravens 30 to 0. To add another pound of pressure to the game, the Terps had a full roster of thirty kids, whereas the Ravens only boasted a paltry fifteen. That meant every kid on our team was going to have to play nearly the whole game without breaks. I could barely breathe on play-off day. My son, who made up with stamina what he lacked in athletic ability, was going up against a championship team, and my husband had been instrumental in getting him there.

Noah asked for assurances from Matt as to what would happen on game day.

"Dad? What's going to happen today?"

"Well, bud, we're going to do the best we can do, and we're going to trust the Lord for the outcome because He knows what's going to happen, and what's best."

This answer didn't satisfy Noah, who wanted the concrete and predictable. Who always does, because the lack of circumstantial control is a torment to his soul. Who was given to exactly the right mother, because she needs to learn to let go too.

"But Dad, you've told me we were going to beat certain teams, and we did! What about today? Can't you tell me if we'll win or lose?"

In one of those impeccable parenting moments, the kind of moment which I knew Matt was capable of before he had ever held one of his own children, he knelt down in front of Noah:

"Son, you can't control winning or losing. The only thing we can control is our own effort and hard work. The Lord knows that, and He wants only the best that you can give

Him. That's what we're going to focus on today. We focus on the things we can control."

When game day arrived as a windy morning in October, Matt and Noah left the house early to prep at the field. I followed later with Jesse and Grace, plying them with hot chocolate and popcorn so I could focus on the game. Jared, the Ravens' head coach and a dear friend of Matt's, was as cool as ice during warm-ups. He is the yin to Matt's yang, which is probably why they get along so well. I'm sure there were moments during the season that Matt would have spontaneously combusted without a cooler head to remind my very competitive husband that it was all "for the kids." Jared supported Matt through the whole season, and my guess is that, because he is humble and possessed of a gentle spirit, he had no awareness of that fact.

As the kickoff approached, one of the players was crying in the parking lot prior to the game, saying he didn't want to be "sat on" because his opponent outweighed him by a good fifty pounds. The kids chattered like squirrels on the sideline, punctuating their pregame hype with some jumping and stretching. Both teams were announced, with the Ravens making dramatic entrances. Every kid had an individual dance that was a variation of something they'd seen a pro football player do during some game, somewhere. Our Ravens certainly did not lack for bravado.

The Terps, however, came on as a team and rushed to the 50-yard line as one mass of prepubescent energy. To our little team of misfits, it was just as intimidating as it was meant to be.

Then the whistle blew.

In the first play of the game, the Terps ran the ball 40 yards. My hand flew to my mouth. "Already?" I choked to one of the mothers next to me. But a few minutes later, the Terps fumbled, and the defense recovered the ball. My breath was coming in short, shallow spurts. I couldn't stand in the bleachers anymore. I started pacing the sideline in tandem with Matt. The Ravens took the recovered ball and drove it down the field. They backed the Terps up, but couldn't score. The first quarter ended with double zeroes on the scoreboard.

But at the end of the second quarter, the Ravens' running back broke through for a 35-yard touchdown. Parents were jumping up and down in hysterics, high-fiving each other and yelling themselves hoarse. By halftime, it was 6 to 0, Ravens. Grace asked me for more hot chocolate, and I threw some bills at her.

"Take your brother!" I yelled as I paced.

As halftime drew to a close, Matt leaned over the fence to me.

"They're exhausted." His face was drawn, and he had his lips pulled tight and flat the way he does when he doesn't think things are going to turn out.

"No!" I retorted. "They'll be fine! Just trust the work you've all put in." But the look on his face already spelled defeat.

As the second half started, the Ravens' kicker kicked the ball. But like a top, it flew ten yards forward, and then bounced backward five yards, catapulting toward the Ravens. The Terps dove in and recovered. Matt told me later he felt it was a foreshadowing of the rest of the game.

We learned that Matt's premonition was right, and the Ravens' players were indeed as tired as he had thought. The season had pushed them as far as they could physically go, and they had nothing left to give. Little by little, the Terps pulled away. With such a large roster, they rotated players in and out by the minute. Everyone came onto the field fresh and aggressive. Though they left everything they had on the field, the Ravens were ultimately overcome. Despite the flushed cheeks of valiant effort, the sweaty heads and tear-soaked faces of little kids who'd given their all, the underdog had indeed been outdone.

Matt and Noah attempted stoicism after the game. But it was a good week before either could talk about it without choking up. They had been waiting for the happily-ever-after that never came.

It seemed to all of us vastly, cosmically unfair.

～

It is no small task to convince a child with his own internal reality that it's ultimately the effort that matters. Even I don't understand why the Lord doesn't guarantee me the desired outcome when I've worked so hard to achieve it. Yet through Noah's own struggles, I am learning about persistence, dedication, and hard work, and of the value they have in and of themselves. When I see Noah sweating on the football field, running sprints with his arms dangling at his sides, my heart bursts with pride. What he wins will not distinguish him as an adult. What he does to achieve a win, will. I am leaning on him in this way. He supports me unknowingly. He supports me by his own willingness to keep on going and not throw himself down on the football field and scream in a raging tantrum. Even when I want to do it for him.

As I write, we are in a new season of football, with a parcel of new lessons being unwrapped at least three times a week. Sometimes, the lessons are on the nature of gracious victory. Sometimes, they are on showing valor in the face of defeat. I can hear Noah in the next room with his siblings, fresh from a bath where he holds his head under the scalding running water and lets the noise and pressure remind him of where he is in space and time. He will soon eat his second bowl of oatmeal (what he loves to call a "midnight snack" even though it's 8:30 p.m., a designation he picked because "I thought you'd get a kick out of it, Mom"). Tonight, this bowl will follow two helpings of lasagna, two pieces of garlic bread, broccoli, and two bottles of Gatorade. But he'll sleep well, once he and his brother stop picking at each other. This will require a few threats from Matt or me, shouted down through the floor register in our bedroom, where, above their fray, we will have to press our hands over our mouths to stifle laughter, because being given a window into the world of two young brothers on the spectrum is equal parts hilarious and miraculous. That will take about ten minutes. Then those extra-large teeth—the Chiclet teeth inherited from his father—will be half hidden by lips parted in sleep, and I will be grateful for the expenditure of energy and the structure of a game he has learned to play better every day; a game through which Daddy supported him and taught him to stand upright in the face of disappointment.

Loner-ism is fairly awful for a life within biblical community. I tried that to no great success in my earlier, unshackled years, in part because I am a bit of a hermitess. People, in large volume, wear me out.

Matt? Matt is P.T. Barnum to our family circus. He is the doorman with the wide smile, master griller in summer, carol singer at Christmas. He is the inviter, the bringer, the extender so that there is always another at the table. We had prayed early in our marriage that God might make our home to reflect Him, that He might make us "fishers of men" (Matt. 4:19 ESV). We didn't anticipate how the Lord would keep stocking the pond.

Into our house came teenage girls fearing unwed pregnancies, drug addicts losing the will to live, couples on the verge of divorce, men with violent pasts. There were college grads with career crises, parents of kids with disabilities, and women struggling quietly with mental illness. It is a fascinating thing to see whom the Lord brings in when one's door is flung wide.

My limits were stretched by my irrepressible, large-living, extrovert husband. I was learning to build others up and shut off my own whining for a while. When I realized the depth of pain these people were experiencing, I was able to put aside my burdens for their benefit. Pain is such a personal thing that it proved harder than I thought to give it up. Putting someone's needs ahead of your own is a simple enough concept. But it required many practiced years before I was fully comfortable with it. My selfishness springs eternal.

However, I was not in any way prepared to ask for help in return. Aside from an introversion that naturally led me to be quiet and self-sufficient (when the hours with guests stretched late into the night, I finally mustered the ability to push past a sense of duty and excuse myself for bed, but was not able to do so until ten years into our marriage), I felt there was a perceived weakness to dependency. I could help others, but I needed no help from anyone else. Which is pretty jacked up if you ask me. And also, kind of arrogant.

The rationale: I didn't want to seem needy. That was my thinking before my ability toward cogent thought deteriorated in the forty-eight hours following my brother's death. I was a weepy, mumbling fool who was trying to keep it together in front of my kids so I could find a bathroom in which to have a brief daily breakdown. There was no way I was going to be able to put one foot in front of the other without some help, so the fear of being "needy" flew right out the window, along with my rational mind. And I discovered that sometimes the leaning on someone, the utter dependence for nearly every need, takes place in one's own house, where the knowing of things about a person, the studying of them, and the loving of them helps you support them in ways you didn't know would be called upon when you stood, absent of gray hair and wrinkles in front of a pastor with a southern drawl, dreamily contemplating how this was the start of the rest of your life. And it is the start of the rest of your life, then. It's also the precursor of all the crap that goes with it. But my husband takes his wedding vows seriously. Though I'm sure he had no idea how he'd eventually be called upon to prove it.

In those days after Sam's death, Matt rose to the occasion with such strength and grace that the further I am removed from it, the more supernatural it seems. I asked him later where he drew the ability from, what part of his history gave him the knowledge to be a pillar to a wife who was falling down.

"It's easy," he said. "You did the same for me when my dad died."

I don't remember such perfection of service to him, but I do remember that when we were newly married, Matt told me his father, who was very ill, would be alive only long enough to see the birth of our son. He told me the Lord had told him this so that he would be prepared and could make the most of every moment with his dad. At the time, I was neither pregnant nor knew our first child would be a boy. I simply remember standing next to him in a receiving line at his father's wake with a three-month-old Noah strapped to my chest in a baby sling, hot and hormonal and emotional, thinking there wasn't anything I could do to lift Matt's terrible burden. But my husband reminds me that I sat with the other sisters-in-law and worked through funeral arrangements with his mother; I reviewed the life insurance policies, and assessed his father's belongings, and helped his mother find a new house. Because that's what you do when someone you love is hurting. When they are falling down, you come in to refresh them, and in so doing, are yourself refreshed (Prov. 11:25).

I also helped Matt's mother discover a jar of my father-in-law's hoarded cash that by eyeballing, she believed to be around $200, but was in reality closer to $1,300 (as I had accurately predicted). I really came off as a hero then, though all it really proved was that I could reach up and pull a jar off a closet shelf, and that I would be good at guessing how many jelly beans are in a jar at a carnival.

So it was when we were in California for my brother's funeral that things to my mind that seemed impossible were, for my husband, a matter of simply picking up the phone. He made travel arrangements and worked with the pastor on the program. He found us places to eat and to rest. And because my precious brother had had a bagpiper at his wedding (as had I, and as my uncle, who also died of lymphoma, had had at his own funeral), my husband picked up the phone and in ten minutes was able to arrange for Eric Rigler, the piper who had played at Ronald Reagan's funeral, to also play at my brother's. I don't know how this happened. It was improbable, certainly, but Matt knew in that moment what to do when the rest of us did not.

This is when I believe there is some magic to Matt's connectivity with other people. I once saw him talk a guard into letting us backstage at the Kennedy Center so my parents could meet conductor and composer Marvin Hamlisch (he of multiple movie scores, Broadway scores, and EGOT-winning fame) on their joint sixtieth birthdays. We brushed past columnist Cal Thomas and Supreme Court Justice Sonia Sotamayor to do it. Behind the velvet ropes and a closed door, Matt extended an arm to Mr. Hamlisch, and then turned to my parents: "Mom and Dad, I'd like you to meet my friend, Marvin Hamlisch." His grin that day, part surprised, part impish and self-impressed, is not something I'll soon forget.

Matt has always supported me. He does, to this day. The thing with grief is that it's generally a silent and surprising visitor. You don't know it's there until you're sitting with your kids on the couch watching Disney's *Frozen*, and the act of true love on screen turns out not to be a kiss between the hero and heroine but a sacrifice between siblings, and you find yourself flying to the bedroom to have a cry that's powerful enough to burst a blood vessel under your eye, making you look like you're in some kind of mothers' fight club. That was two months past Sam's death. Never since then have I ever had a moment of sorrow to which Matt hasn't entitled me and given me the space and protection to experience. Though sometimes, Grace likes to sneak in the bedroom when I'm mourning, and tells me to look at her because she "likes the way I look when I cry." And this is clearly a whole different thing that I'm going to have to address with her, or that she will be addressing on her own in therapy, because it mostly leads to her crying too, as I'm not always in the best position to "make it better" when I'm facedown in a pile of my own snot.

I look back on the aftermath of my brother's death and wonder at the sideshow that was our life and all that had to be coordinated to get to California in seventy-two hours. Here is where all the supporting of others came to bear, somehow. It was as if every little kindness I had shown to those in our lives had been stored up and rolled out gracefully and in perfect syncopation when it was most needed. There were the kids, all three of them, with school schedules and after-school sports. My friends Michelle, Karen (a former neighbor), and Mandy (Coach Jared's wife) handled that. There were the animals: two dogs, two cats, horses, guinea pigs, and hermit crabs. My friend Becky stepped in to watch them and to oversee the house. Matt's boss stepped up by extending condolences and deadlines, and even the largest snowstorm of the season couldn't waylay those who were determined to show us love. At one point, Michelle was barricaded in a snowbound house with her two children, plus my three, and both her dog and one of mine. If she was losing her mind, she never let on. During our absence, all I got were tender messages from her asking how I was.

Meals arrived, flowers appeared, cards poured in. I was overwhelmed by the crush of love from people we had, somewhere in our history, been privileged to love on as well. For this is what biblical community is, isn't it? It is the peace that comes through sacrifice, and the strength that comes from support. It is being Christ to others by dying to self. It is encouraging one another and building each other up, just as we were doing before our own foundations were shaken (1 Thess. 5:11). For every one of us is leaning under the weight of some burden. When we stand tallest is when we hold someone else up for a while.

9

Mind Control
and Major Mom

See, LORD, how distressed I am! I am in torment within, and in my
heart I am disturbed.

Lamentations 1:20

So here we come to the hardest part.

The external stuff, and all that's needed by the little people
around you in abundance, every day; that detritus of a mother's life requiring constant management—that is not the most
difficult thing, though it is more than enough, if one has it. For
the unfortunate few of us (or perhaps, a few million?), there
is an internal dialogue that proves trickier than negotiating
anything else in the chaos of this journey.

How does one reconcile the heart and the mind? And what if the mind refuses to cooperate? What if the knowing of the right things doesn't actually lead to the management of things?

What if you're in the well and you can't get out?

I fought Matt for a year on the concept of getting a mother's helper. It strikes me now as humorous that my well-intentioned husband was insistent on getting me help with the kids, and I was insistent on refusing it. These are the kinds of fights we have now, this revised pair of us who has seen so much. Matt will tell you that he is usually trying to do something for my own good, and I'm usually trying to foil his efforts. I might lose a foot to gangrene if it weren't for my husband's insistence that I perform regular self-maintenance. Like going to the doctor to get a nail fungus treated. I'm generally content just to let something eat my foot and bear it all with a stiff upper lip. On my own, of course.

I'll call this young woman a mother's helper, but she's really a babysitter. I've always thought mother's helper sounded more benign, like I'm there lending a hand around every corner. But I'm not. Sometimes, I actually leave the house. And anyway, if I were available at all times, there wouldn't be much point to having someone there to help. Whatever you call this sweet-faced twentysomething, I didn't initially want her. Singularly maintaining a house and kids (two of whom were on the spectrum) and writing and being sick, all with a traveling husband—this was the hallmark of a good wife, I thought. I had to have everything locked down, perfectly managed. As it turns out, all it makes for is a shrieking harpy.

With no family in the area, and children who often refused to sleep, I became a grumbling, edgy version of my former self. Needing childcare help is also, I'm certain, a function of not having your first baby until you're thirty. When you're finally done ushering little people into the world by thirty-six, you're not really getting a full night's sleep until you're forty which, unless you're Jennifer Aniston, is middle-aged. And also very, very tired, and very, very broke because you end up spending whatever the going rate is for childcare help, plus generally a premium because you live out in "God's country." I also learned why multiple generations lived together in the same house at the turn of the century. Crowded? Yes. But our ancestors had figured out how to propagate their own babysitters. And my uterus told me in no uncertain terms that was not an option. I think I actually heard it laugh. As did my parents. And Matt's mother. And all other relations who were propositioned to move in so we could get some help. Apparently, the people of the twenty-first century value their personal space.

So I began to slowly dispatch with the idea of a perfectly controlled life. I learned the laundry could be "done" simply by closing the laundry room door, that takeout qualified as "dinner," and that if I said "no" to a social commitment, the earth would not open up and swallow me whole. I accepted a "mother's helper" because I knew we were without extended family, in the middle of nowhere, with three small children who needed more of me than my tank of reserves could pour out at one time. I admitted my need for assistance, but I didn't say I was happy about it.

In fact, there are some times I'm not happy about anything.

The sympathetic nervous system that had so plagued me in early adulthood—that fight-or-flight, scan-the-horizon, quivering apprehension of my rabbit psyche—kicked into high gear once I became a mother. The fact that I have two boys who at any minute are trying to escape or kill each other, or screaming about clothing or food doesn't help an autonomic response geared toward reacting to strife or emergency. Everything feels like an emergency for someone with brain wiring like mine, even when it's not. "If I can just stress about it enough," I repeat to myself, "then the desired outcome will ensue!" I think this whole account proves I'm so skilled at repetition I might win an award for it. But then I'd just make myself anxious about not winning.

I've passed this nifty gene on to my son Noah, who, on the way to a recent birthday party at a LEGO store, was practically apoplectic thinking he had missed the toy-building portion of the party.

He was rocking frantically in the backseat.

"Have they started yet?"

"How close are we?"

"Drive faster!"

He's also anxious because high-functioning autistics have a higher index of anxiety than other children their age.[1]

Before our arrival at the party, when we circled our packed car through a mall parking lot on a Saturday and Noah began to let loose the tears he hates to release, Matt and I knew he was at maximum capacity. Contrast this with his father who can cry on a dime, and for whom a head bow and quivering lip portend a flood of tears. But there is something of a beautiful contrast in a man the size and strength of a linebacker (I will brag on him a little here and say he's deadlifted over 450 lbs. after that shoulder surgery of his) showing tenderness and sensitivity. What I love about this also is that it shows our children that it's OK to be vulnerable.

Now, I'm not one for this type of demonstration, myself. I would rather put on a pair of oversized sunglasses and laugh it off than I would let you see me blubber. What I know to be true, that Jesus Himself wept (John 11:35), further proves how graceless I am with myself. I do not permit myself the expression of the most human of emotions, not even the ones Christ exhibited Himself in the fullness of His own God-humanity. Which is the downswing of this psychological rhythm I've got. I run and angst and fret. I turn my face from yours if my cheeks are hot with tears. I bury the hurt-ish things and squash all the ugly stuff, so that the ridiculous stuff like the dog kibble being spilled on the floor becomes Chernobyl, and I spark up and send everyone running because a tiny thing has become a catastrophe and I have no reserves left to deal with it, having burned them all up in the maintenance of my anxiety and perceived perfection. I burn every candle in my stash at both ends and do not feel the heat of the flame until I hit the wall hard. Then I'm all burned up, leaving behind a catatonic shell that looks like a wife and mother but really wants to lay her un-showered body in bed all day and watch unsatisfactory TV on dirty sheets and tell the kids that Mommy isn't feeling well.

I discovered early on that anxiety has an end. It cannot run limitlessly. It is finite, as we are. And when it stops, there is no place to go but down, down into the well—into the dark that has followed me for so long. Perhaps it's followed me since high school, when I wanted to be someone other than myself; perhaps since college, when a young therapist told me life was as simple as what I would wear to work.

I also know the dark could very well—*may* very well—be part of my Behcet's. Numerous studies have found a correlation in both anxiety and depression with Behcet's patients,[2] perhaps owing to the cerebral vascular involvement that affects psychological functioning, or the nature of chronic pain on a patient's state of mind. Of course, being sick for a long time with something super rare didn't exactly make me a Pollyanna, either.

I do not know when the dark place in the ground opened up to me. I only know it is where I find myself each time the panic stops.

I sigh the words, repeated so often: "How long must I wrestle with my thoughts and day after day have sorrow in my heart?" (Ps. 13:2). I suspect the poet who penned them, hiding in caves, contemplating his own death, struggled with a great sadness too.

In each of their own ways, my precious children come to me and offer sympathies and well wishes. Noah's cursory "Hope you feel better, Mom," and Jesse's "I will pray for your heart, Mom," are like pantomimes. They are the motion of things only, their representation and not their reality. They have no effect, even when they are delivered at just the right moment, when I need them so badly. Even when they come from children's mouths, with small hands pressed on my face. I cannot explain to them that it is not as easy as "getting over it," so I tell them I will feel better, eventually. I refrain from saying "soon."

Grace of course, bright and intuitive as she is, sees through all the verbal substitution I use, and cuts me sideways with her attention to the thing I'm trying to hide.

Hiding depression is, with her, about as effective as masking a lost limb: "Oh what, this little thing? No worries, it's just a scratch!"

"You're sad again, Mom, aren't you?" she says. I wince, and nod. Then she puts her head next to mine, mashing her purple glasses up against both our faces, and petting me with one hand whose nails bear the remnants of four different polishes. Her hands are also a little dirty, because she refuses to wash them unless I plead smallpox with her. Prepping her for school the other day, I looked at her grubby mitts while I brushed her hair.

"When is the last time you washed your hands, Grace?"

"Hmm. Can't remember, Mom."

Which was odd, because she'd showered the night before and had apparently managed to keep her hands out of the water the whole time.

But I love her little hands on mine and her little heart, so aware and peeking into things that she sees first, before her brothers.

What I hate is when I think my children might feel the density of my illness crushing their own selves, scaring them perhaps, leaving them without answers. I wish I were better at hiding it, but when it comes, it is no use to push the bigness of this weight off my chest in order to spare them. I am like that cartoon coyote again, this time under the anvil, and my efforts are useless.

"Help me get out from under this thing!" I want to scream.

"*Meep Meep!*" my psyche blurts back, and disappears into the dark canyon.

"Well, thanks a lot for leaving me here again for God-knows-how-long, you hateful thing!"

I cannot express fully how hard it is to interact with these beautiful, developing individuals who need you all the time, and for whom you never want a moment of doubt to sprout in their minds about your love for them, because you can already envision them with their own adult struggles and are silently terrified that they will cross their legs in some dimly lit therapist's office one morning in the future, and say, "Well, it all started with my mother . . ." Because if you think about it, then you just might get more depressed.

~

Winston Churchill once wrote, "I don't like standing near the edge of a platform when an express train is passing through. I like to stand right back and if possible get a pillar between me and the train. I don't like to stand by the side of a ship and look down into the water. A second's action would end everything. A few drops of desperation."[3] Churchill wrote later that he struggled with a black dog whose appearance could never be predicted, and whose mastery was never guaranteed. When the "black dog" of his depression appeared, there was little but a gleam of discernible hope preventing Winston Churchill from acting on those drops of desperation. Charismatic, popular, and brilliant with a seeming inability to comprehend impossibility of circumstance, Churchill was later speculated to have been living with bipolar disorder.[4] Yet who but someone that has felt the darkness of an apparently insurmountable obstacle can point legions of others toward the beam of hopeful light in the distance?

What for that world leader was his black dog is, for me, the bottom of my well. And to say I detest falling there would be to underestimate the nature of its horribleness. It would be to distort, by not-huge-enough-characterization, how very frightening it is down there.

When I am in the well, it's me below the surface. This is what I told Matt once that finally made him realize what I experienced when the shadows come. I told him I could see the sky above me, I was conscious of the beam of hopeful light, but there was no bucket and the walls were slick and there wasn't any climbing out. It was, it *is*, like being a part of the same world as everybody else, but not always getting to live on the same plane. Things are going on around me in which my mind can't engage because it's on lockdown with this horrible darkness. Though even the whole time I'm thinking, "You have these great kids and wonderful husband, and you don't want for anything, and there are kids starving in Africa, you ingrate!"

So it's kind of a strange cycle to be in, because even in my depression, I'm kind of depressed about being depressed in the first place, like I'm not entitled to a chemical imbalance because other people have it worse off than me.

A combination of heredity (all that genetic nonsense in my crooked DNA) and environment sets off some kind of mismanagement of normally existing chemicals so that they either show up in droves like a bus full of tweens headed to a Justin Beiber concert, or in some weird catalytic reaction, they're sucking exhaust and running behind the rest of my brain in a desperate, unsuccessful attempt to catch up. I once had someone tell me medicine is "for people who can't get their [expletive] together." Which was odd, considering this person's impressive level of dysfunction. She did not know about my psychic struggles, and I never told her. In what may seem a contradiction to my earlier statement about my being part of a culture of confession, I did not feel compelled to reveal this part of my construct. Without her realizing it, she had illegitimated a part of me: that very real struggle of mine and of many other people that exists and torments and wounds us. It would have been like pointing to and remarking on a painting on the wall, while the person next to you tells you that the painting is not actually there. It felt pointless to be transparent about this with someone like that.

I am comforted to some extent in that I share the plight of this occasional well-dwelling with some of the world's most beautiful and luminous minds, including Van Gogh, Beethoven, Abraham Lincoln, Theodore Roosevelt, Sylvia Plath, Mark Twain, Virginia Woolf, Frida Khalo, and Edgar Allan Poe. I like to joke with Matt that maybe being a little bit sadder also makes me a little bit wiser. Being slightly off-kilter could be good for original thought: perhaps we sad sacks tap a pocket of brainpower that perpetually happy people don't always get to. I play the "tortured artist" card with him a lot.

Even as I clack away on these keys, I feel like my ugly scab is being picked away, and I'm letting open a part of me that cardinally draws into consideration some of the wrongheaded notions that persist, even in the church, about mental illness and depression. But tragedy strikes us too, as we learned in the wake of the Matthew Warren tragedy: when the son

of a famous pastor, who by all accounts had a thriving relationship with Jesus Christ, could no longer shoulder the
burden of his own disorder and succumbed to it by taking
his own life. Matthew was not "cursed" or "in sin" any more
than my autistic son is when he has a panic attack, because
it falls under the umbrella of a neurobiological diagnosis
God saw fit to permit for him; because it is a physiological
disorder; because the brain is a physical organ just like the
heart, the thyroid, or the liver. Autism or bipolar disorder or
schizophrenia or depression or ADHD result from chemical
imbalances in the brain—faulty wiring, if you will. In fact,
neuroimaging confirms the interior changes that result in
these types of diagnoses.[5] Diseases of the mind are simply
diseases of an organ like any other.

"His disciples asked him, 'Rabbi, who sinned, this man or
his parents, that he was born blind?' 'Neither this man nor
his parents sinned,' said Jesus, 'but this happened so that
the works of God might be displayed in him'" (John 9:2–3).

Perhaps we too—my sons and I—are constructed such that
the works of God might be displayed in us, we humble be-
ings, who sometimes find ourselves at the bottom of the well.

~

Then comes Christmas: a holiday sated with satisfaction,
with food and music, gifts and parties, the penultimate cel-
ebration of the whole year, where happiness is as plentiful
as fruitcake.

What do you, the afflicted, do about Christmas?

What do you do when there are so many expectations of
so many (and of your oldest in particular) and they are all

so pressing? These expectations that, if unmet, will cause the air to be sucked out of the room before it all explodes with a tantrum, like that scene in *Backdraft* where the awful hissing whine precedes a rumble, and eventually the whole thing blows up? When one of you is anxious about getting the "right" thing to put under the tree, and the other is ready to lose it because he doesn't think the "right" thing *is* actually under the tree?

We're quite a pair, me and my oldest boy.

In the chaos of Christmas, when the paper is flying, and you're watching all the effort you've lovingly invested into the presentation of gifts become airborne in a shower of ribbon and tissue, and your son is starting to freak out and yell at you because things aren't moving quickly enough for him, and he is crying because there must be, *there has to be*, a box at the back of the tree into which someone has packed the tablet he has tormented you for this entire season, there is only one thing to do: zip him into a big, blue body suit and back away.

This is what saved our last Christmas.

Not literally, of course. There's naturally the meaning of Christmas. There is its eternality, and the hope of someone Bigger than us giving us His greatest gift, and the love that binds us together when we're forced to share living space for a week with out-of-town relatives (especially when you run out of toilet paper). There's that important thing.

But what actually salvaged the morning of Christmas itself looked more like something you'd find in a coroner's office than something you'd love discovering under the tree. I raised my hands in a silent "hallelujah" when Noah pulled it from the gift bag I offered him during his meltdown, because I knew what would happen next. If I'm being honest, I was also raising my hands in an "I told you!" gesture to my husband, who suggested, judiciously and for good reason, that perhaps a Lycra body suit wasn't on every nine-year-old's wish list.

Noah's eyes were welling with tears and each little thing—a sweater, or a toy, or a board game—was sending his anxiety skyward. I could hear his brain churning: "What if I don't get the tablet I want! Oh no! I told Santa, and it was on my list! And if I don't get it, then that means Santa doesn't really exist, and if he doesn't exist, Mom and Dad have been lying to me the whole time, and I am the victim of a great and terrible conspiracy! Alternatively, if I don't get it, it means he exists, but he's determined that I've been bad this year, not good! And I am a terrible person who is therefore unworthy of a tablet and . . . *argh*!"

This is how it goes. A little bit upset, mind out of control, a lot bit upset, repeat (yes, like his mother. So you can stop smirking). So I grabbed the package with the body suit in it.

Noah took it out and fingered in silence the heavy, stretchy material. Then he noticed the Velcro front. He did not need to be instructed on what to do next. Wordlessly, he unhooked the tabs, and stepped in. Then he asked if I would close it up. And when I did, Noah got down onto the floor—right there in the living room among the fireplace and the presents, over the smell of coffee and the sound of laughter, in the midst of every stimulant that had sent his nervous system into overdrive—and he curled up into a little ball and was quiet.

That was how the body sock saved Christmas.

Now it sits in a heavy puddle in his desk drawer for easy access. Sometimes I find Noah inside it, completely enclosed, playing with the tablet that had once caused him so much distress. It is among his most treasured possessions because it told him without telling him, that I knew what he needed. It told my little boy in the blue body suit that, without a specific request from him, I could give him the thing he wanted most: a quiet, darkened space that would help him find a level track for his always-sprinting mind. For that, I thank the Lord, and the intuition with which He has so graciously bestowed me.

I also thank Amazon.com.

After the New Year, what was a much-prayed-for-and-saved-for Christmas gift became, as per usual, a source of obsession for our son. This is an area in which ASD kids truly excel: when they take hold of an object (or person or idea), getting them to let go of it is like trying to Jell-O wrestle a cat. The pursuit of specific and narrow areas of interest is one of the most striking features of Asperger's syndrome. "Serial obsessions," our neurologist calls them. Obsessive-compulsive disorder is analogous, and characterized by a pervasive preoccupation with perfectionism, orderliness, and control. The one is a differential diagnosis for the other. But they are distinguishable enough that when your son carries both, every day is ripe with opportunities to go to battle with a very determined spirit.

I believe it's been established that I hate to fight.

By the time we were into day four of Noah's new gift, I was already dreading asking him to get dressed, eat a meal, do his homework, or take a shower because each directive elicited a scream. Not a begrudging moan or a reluctant surrender, but a sobbing howl because he couldn't let it go. He would bend over the tablet like a penitent monk, playing each game until it was mastered and he could move to the next level. Mastery, and as quick as possible, was his ultimate goal. I began to dread approaching him about routine tasks.

And it wasn't just Noah who was engrossed in his tablet, it was Jesse as well. Jesse and Grace had also received tablets for Christmas. I freely admit these were self-serving gifts. Matt and I had wanted to ensure we could bypass hours of screaming about gift inequity and how much Noah had to share with his siblings. For Jesse, the tablet ushered in hour after hour of documentaries on pro wrestlers. Match after televised match, rehashed online. Dialogues of dominance memorized and repeated ("I am the heavyweight champion of the world!" said John Cena; "I'm the heavyweight champion of the world!" said Jesse, who, by this point, had also taken off his shirt and found a pair of plastic dog tags to replicate the aforementioned Mr. Cena).

"Noah, can you please go downstairs and get your pj's on?"

"Mom! I'm almost at the next level!" (flinging self on floor)

"Jesse, you have to put the tablet down to brush your teeth. You can pick it up again after you've brushed your teeth."

"I hate brushing my teeth!" (stomping away) *"Hate it!"* (screaming)

By this point, my ears were usually bleeding.

Because fear is the most prevalent emotion of autism, I had to tease out the anxiety from within the fixation. So many sources of original joy in the boys' lives have crossed the line into obsessive preoccupation. But their roots are almost always found in fear.

I can't imagine where they get this.

Oh, wait. Yes I can.

My husband was kind enough to point out to me that lately I've taken a love of my own to a level of utter radicalism—surfing the internet for information, talking about it incessantly, lying awake at night ruminating on it. This wasn't a gentle admonition, either. Matt came right out and called me obsessed. So I plumbed my own psyche for the obsession's cause and discovered that I'm afraid I will never get this thing. Ever. Because I've wanted it five times longer than Noah's been alive. And when you've waited that long, well, it's hard not to think the universe is playing a cruel joke by not letting you have it.

Just yesterday, this verse appeared on my phone through my "Daily Bible" application: "The mind governed by the flesh is death, but the mind governed by the Spirit is life and peace" (Rom. 8:6). When you're struggling with questions of mental peace and, out of 31,100 verses in the Bible, this particular one shows up on your phone, it's hard not to feel the hem of the Lord's cloak as He passes by.

My desires, Noah's desires, all of our desires, are fleshly. Which isn't to say "ungodly." You see, I think God puts good things in our lives that we continue to want, and then provides them for us when He determines it's good to do so. But when those good things become "every waking minute" things, the spirit has been given over to the flesh. It may not be easy telling Noah or Jesse to take a break. But I suppose that puts me in the role of chief exposure officer. Like the way people with arachnophobia are pushed toward a cure by being thrown into a room full of spiders. I show the uncomfortable thing by doing the uncomfortable thing myself. Like when Matt yells, "Get off the computer!" Because I don't really want to take a break, either. In fact, I just want to basically push things as far as I possibly can, until I hit that brick wall and find myself once again at the bottom of the well.

~

When Noah or Jesse is overtired, there is no self-regulation in either of them (as is often the case for kids with autism spectrum disorder), so they will run until their legs can carry them no farther and their lungs are set to burst with effort. These boys will seem perfectly modulated one minute, and then the next, they're on the floor screaming, terrorizing each other with extra force, refusing the simplest of tasks. We had, one particular night, mentioned the prospect of a small change, with opportunities for all the kids to weigh in. Just bringing it up set Noah to sobbing.

As for me? Well, I too was exhausted on the day this change was mentioned. After hosting a birthday party for Jesse on Saturday that lasted well into the night with flashlight tag, Matt and I unloaded the entirety of our portable storage unit. Every last box, bin, toy, and piece of furniture. I managed to bruise my shin and torque my elbow, and the next day, I crawled my aching body to the bed for a two-hour nap with Jesse.

I might have left it at that. I knew I was overtired. Instead, I put on my riding boots and went out into the field to get the pony and our thoroughbred mare, who both needed training and feeding. After I finally cornered the pony, who made me chase him a good twenty minutes before capture, in a moment of misplaced confidence I swung a leg over him in the field, intending to ride him bareback into the barn for our session.

This action was based in part on the frequent social media posts I encounter by young teenage girls I know, relative to how they ride their horses and ponies bareback, with nothing more than a halter and a lead rope. However, I am not a teenager. Also, this pony was not the quiet packer type. These are both key distinctions. Therefore, the minute I got on the fat pony who looks—quite benignly—like an oversized stuffed animal with a long face and doe eyes and flowing, reddish mane, I instantly regretted it.

The pony swung his head around to look at me. I could nearly sense him taking into account my age and fitness level and unsteadiness on his back. Then, he rocked back on his haunches and took off galloping toward the rest of the herd, with me clutching like a monkey to his long mane. This farce didn't last long. In a moment that seemed like it would last forever, but was in reality probably half a second, I was swinging over his shoulder, and my un-teenage body was shuttling toward the hard, hard ground.

The impact was too much for me to handle, and mentally adding it to a long list of second-guesses that are the tattoos of well-dwelling ("This, too, is doomed to fail!"), I just rolled over in the alfalfa and started sobbing. Jesse called from the barn, "Mama, are you OK? I will call Daddy for you!" I half lifted a hand and moaned, "No . . . I'm . . . OK. Just give me a minute!"

The Lord must have heard my feeble misery from on high, because He decided to step in. As I lay in the dirt, whimpering and picking gnats off my lip, I heard a snuffling sound. I felt something on my head and looked up. There around me in a near-circle were all six horses in the field who had come to stand next to me after I'd fallen. Mozart, the largest and a famed steeplechaser in his day, had rested his impressive muzzle on my head, as if to ask if I was all right. After a good ten minutes of self-pity, I could feel the Lord shepherd me back to the house in the form of my little Jesse, who held my hand and asked if he could take me to the hospital in his ambulance. Then, when we finally got back into the house, I felt the Lord stifling a laugh when I fell on the floor crying in Matt's office, telling him what had happened and that I felt like a failure because I hadn't pulled off the bareback riding scene from *The Black Stallion*.

Jesse jumped right in: "You can do it, Mom! You're still young!"

"Young" is relative to Jesse of course, as he believes the babysitters we hire to be the same age as Matt and me, and every time they arrive, it becomes harder and harder to explain that there is a good twenty-plus years between me and them.

Matt helped me up off the floor and looked at me. Then he took my face in his hands, and said, "I have total confidence in you. I love you, and I believe in you. You are still a great rider, bareback or not."

I heard it in the same way he heard me say to him once, "There's no one I'd rather carry a dead dog with than you." It was the sort of thing you remember in times of future difficulty, the kind of thing you remember because it's exactly what your heart needs, and it is true.

I have learned that humility comes before honor (Prov. 18:12). And who else is more humble than s/he who cries after being tossed off the back of a naughty pony? Jesus himself cried at Lazarus's death—because of His own personal loss and the great love He had for His friend. To be sure, Jesus had quite a few more reasons to cry than I did after "ponygate." But I know for certain He is one acquainted with our sufferings—a "man of sorrows" who was despised by many (Isa. 53:3 NLT). Sorrow is, after all, a perfectly acceptable state of mind; it isn't shameful and needn't be hidden. Even if our state of mind is one of increased fragility, and the pain is deeper than usual, or the body hurts a little too much, we are known by a God who understands our tears, who loves us despite of and because of them.

I still try not to cry. But if a few tears happen to slip out, I'm less peeved at my own "weakness." Especially when the Lord sends horses to comfort me as I cry.

~

Parenting children on the spectrum is always a blessing. Noah's and Jesse's powers of observation bring to light things I would never have ordinarily noticed. Their satellites are always spinning, and the effect is an accumulation of things that changes my perspective. They are, like many high-functioning autistics, gatherers of things. Jesse's "gadget cabinet" is a wonder: there are toy weapons, and parts of things that once worked, and wrestling figurines, and many, many Mardi Gras beads. Noah's corner shelf is stuffed full. In it are a dead beetle, a LEGO "man" created entirely of heads, an empty paper bag stood upright, and multiple shark teeth.

However, their observational strengths can be quite challenging. Especially when they involve conversations like this:

"Mom—you've got to get that trampoline out of the yard." (A windstorm—typical in our previous neighborhood of a few years ago, where in a high-elevation, breezy country area we lacked protection from a tree line—had demolished our trampoline, sending it flying over our fence. There it hung, like a deflated metal balloon, to the chagrin of all our neighbors, until we could get to it with a hacksaw.)

"I know, Noah."

"And our mailbox is just hanging open—it won't close! And the console in the car is broken, and that side part [siding] of the house, I mean we should just paint it . . . and this place looks like a junkyard!"

As if I hadn't already felt the blight of the disrepair around our house. Now my son had gathered a list of our possessions' deficits and reminded me that together, everything looked subpar. The irony here was that Noah then refused (and still refuses) to clean his room. Which means that our previous home's "junkyard" extended everywhere but up the stairs and down the hallway. I'm of a belief that Noah and Jesse share this in common with every other little boy.

So, whose reality was Noah's perception? If I see things through Noah's eyes, am I seeing them as they really are? After all, Noah cannot perceive sarcasm, or figures of speech, or accurately assess the more subtle emotions in others. And so his statement that our home was a "junkyard" might have been true for him—it may accurately represent what he thought—but may not have accurately represented the state of affairs.

It's hard to turn off that mother-habit of believing all that your child says. But children don't always believe the things that are actually true. They may believe that there are

207

monsters in the closet or that they can fly. Or that, despite the fact that they know they are permitted only one snack after dinner, they are capable of bamboozling their long-suffering grandfather into giving them two snacks because "That's the rule. Mommy says so." Grace, for example, believed once that if she didn't have the requisite number of brown and black caterpillars she would never have a friend again, as these bugs had become some kind of mean girl currency at school. I am happy to report she is surviving just fine with more friends than she can keep up with. Each new party invitation causes me to stare morosely at my checkbook.

I am learning to swap believing for knowing. I try to step back from my unhappy circumstances when they come and accurately assess what is true, rather than what feels true. I am helping my kids to do it too. I endeavor to understand my children better with every day, to walk a mile in their shoes. But I also endeavor to be someone who "believe[s] *and* who know[s] the truth" (1 Tim. 4:3, emphasis added). Someone who knows, for example, that our home is not a junkyard. Though we did eventually remove the trampoline.

It was laid to rest in an actual junkyard.

~

My default was once a distrust of my own decisions. I could make a federal case of the choice of movie, outfit, or ice cream flavor, assuming that self-destruction was the natural corollary of the wrong decision. But God is changing my personal mistrust through my children, and especially my boys who, as a function of what they have, trust absolutely everyone. Grace understands "stranger danger." For the boys, it's "stranger handshake" and a "Wanna come to my house?" That part might not be from autism, actually. It might be from their father.

We're told to be "wise as serpents and innocent as doves" (Matt. 10:16 ESV), and that if we desire wisdom, we have only to ask our Father for it, and it will be freely given (James 1:5). Though I was matched with criticism in the early stages of this journey with my atypical sons, I persisted in the difficult task of reaching a diagnosis for them both because the Lord gave me what I prayed for: discernment. Our neurologist has applauded our efforts toward early intervention, saying that most high-functioning children on the spectrum aren't diagnosed until they are seven or eight. Noah was five. Jesse was three. Matt jokes I am beset with a certain level of paranoia. I tell him for the 5 percent that it pays off, it's worth it.

In trusting God, I have also learned to trust myself. I have learned to listen to His voice within me, quiet though it may be, and appreciate the mother radar that He's tuned to just the right frequency.

I have also learned to wait for the bucket that I know He will toss down into the well, and which will bring me up and back into the light.

10

Exit Strategy

Who is wise and understanding among you? Let them show it by their good life, by deeds done in the humility that comes from wisdom.

James 3:13

I've spent a lot of time feeling like that kid on the playground who hit the asphalt because the bigger kid thinks it's hilarious to kick her knees out from under her. I've had my share of disability, hardship, and loss. They've forced my peace with chaos, and a wisdom born only of experience. And man, am I wise. Humble too. Not in a "wasn't that funny I called myself humble after saying I was wise?" kind of way, but in the "I know what I know because I've seen a lot" kind of way. You get like that when the Lord brings the fire of experience to your doorstep. But I don't regret it. I wouldn't return it to

Him who brought it, because all of it has taught us how to act humbly, to rely on Him, to accept the unstructured form of the start-to-finish of our lives. The tidier things are, the harder it is to rely on God. So I would still take all of it, all over again.

Autism is the thing that hangs around, the one on the list that there is no "getting over," no "curing," because, as our doctor reminded us, "even the term *high-functioning* is a bit of a misnomer. The boys will only ever learn to manage their autism. Their brains are permanently and distinctly different from yours." Autism therefore means everything to us in that it pervades every moment of every day. It is an experience from which I do not get a break. It is the silent question behind the taunting kids at school ("Is it because Noah's different?"), the quiet realization behind every self-stimulating behavior, the knowledge of what sets them off, the "it's too loud for him," or "there are too many people here," or "he does not like the feel of my hugs" thoughts. It is everything in every moment of every day with my children, including the middle one who is on this roller coaster too, even though she, like her parents, didn't sign on for it.

But these developmental disabilities and the burdens that follow also mean nothing. These diagnoses are a part of them, and not their wholes. They are the "this is what he has, not who he is," and the "I don't think I'd want him any other way" ideations that rattle through my heart each day I spend with them. It is the refusal to make excuses for them, and the toeing of a hard line, and the working to make things the best they can possibly be because an ICD-9 code and the *DSM* don't have a clue what they're like in real life. These "disabilities" mean nothing. The Lord has called my children to something great because of what they've been dealt, and in spite of it. It's nothing they can't handle, and apparently nothing I can't handle, despite what I think and how it feels. When I look up, He gives me what I need, every time.

All of our messy life has humbled me in a way that only someone who thought they could once control everything can be humbled. Because I now realize, fully and from hard, beautiful experience, that I am not in control of my life. Which is, of course, exactly how it was meant to be.

~

Summer delays its entrance in this wide, greenish space of ours, a space where we live in a rented home for a moment longer without knowing what the future will bring. Here, a broad span of white horse fence, gravel under our tires, and a combine harvester that takes up both lanes of traffic constitute "rush hour." These are the things that accompany a trip to school, when the whining is loudest because the snow days were all used and then some, so the kids are in school when the weather is hot. Sorry, kiddos. Thank the polar vortex.

The neighbor girl on her paint pony brings a petting zoo to our doorstep. When Noah elopes, he is likely somewhere close, because there is much to interest him close to the house. There are horses in the paddock and a little stream into which the three kids like to go adventuring and always come home soaked like naughty retrievers. A field of sheep on the way to school are a certain way to buy a few moments of peace, because God's animals are always a pleasure and a great diversion. And lowing cattle, with the windows down and a "Guys, can you hush for a minute? Listen!" can actually bring the screeching in the backseat to a halt.

There are tractor rides on Halloween in our former neighborhood, where the neighbors are also friends. The geese honk here overhead every day, in all seasons (I don't think they're flying south, but actually in circles). When the dogs bark, it's only at a fox or a deer ambling through the uncut alfalfa in the back field, and not something worse, because I'm pretty sure someone looking to burglarize would get lost on their way out to find us. The open sky and darting swallows, the pond with one lazy turtle, the click of cicadas on a summer night are simple gifts from God. Even as I write this, a herd of deer are meandering with no particular intensity across the lawn in the middle of the day, driving the dogs crazy behind the glass, and making me laugh because their apple-sized brains have somehow comprehended the dogs won't be released to chase them. The little one is practically blowing raspberries.

It's no accident we're in this house, then. It is like the Lord to use wild things, possessed of a lovely disorganization, to remind me that His perfect, ordered design has set them all in motion.

A moment stepping back from this life with its myriad blessings helps me realign my thinking when Noah's pulled the guinea pig out and taken half a cage's worth of shavings with him onto the floor (the floor I just vacuumed yesterday); when I've managed to dessicate the houseplants because I don't have the time to water them, when the check I forget to enter in the register clears the bank and overdraws our account, when I can't see my bed for the unfolded laundry, and when Noah wakes me at 1:00 a.m. to tenderly inquire, "Is there anything I can get you, Mom?" Because what I really want to yell is, "How 'bout some sleep?"

The minute we are born, we are dying. And when I am old, if I persist in living that long, I know I will miss the nighttime creeping that precedes a whispered request to sleep with me. I will miss peeking at our door through a half-closed eye to watch how stealthily one of my children turns the knob, how gently the door is closed. This quietness will always mystify me, for when the sun is in the heavens, my children know only how to *slam* doors.

When I'm old, I will miss the elbows and knees and pointy joints softened by a covering of baby fat that dig their way into my ribs. I will miss the comfort of their presence beside me when Daddy is away on business. I will miss how it brings me peace in a home that is sometimes unfamiliar. I will miss having to pause for my evening's final task—turning on the hall light—so that the path to my room isn't dark or frightening for whoever will be walking there.

When I am old, I will miss the screaming that takes place between two children above my head at three o'clock in the morning, because each wants me to themselves.

Actually, no. I won't miss that at all.

When I am old, I will be the one begging for "a hug and a kiss"—not Jesse, the one for whom I now act as a human security blanket. I will be the one asking if Grace will lie down beside me—not Grace asking me. I will be the one still seeking out a reticent Noah, wrapping my arms around him in the gorilla embrace that is one of the few he tolerates, feeling those hands flapping underneath me like penguin wings.

When I am old, I'll miss the baby breath humming through still, pinkish lips. I'll miss the fuzz of a blanket carried to bed against my face. I'll miss kissing the tops of their heads as they settle in, grinning like monkeys because they've had their way. And the mess too. I will miss that, I am sure.

"Give thanks to the Lord, for he is good; his love endures forever" (1 Chron. 16:34). On the days I forget to thank Him, this perfect and beautiful mess helps me remember.

Ours is a humble life, a good life. Matt and I often ask each other, "Can you believe how good this is?" And the answer is, of course, no.

No, we cannot.

Notes

Chapter 2 Angst and the Type A

1. Joan Didion, "Letter from 'Manhattan,'" *New York Review of Books*, August 16, 1979, http://www.nybooks.com/articles/archives/1979/aug/16/letter-from -manhattan/.
2. Michael Glover, *Wellington as Military Commander* (London: B. T. Batsford, 1968), 205.

Chapter 3 There Must Be Some Mistake

1. Rachel Ewing, Drexel University, Office of Communications, "Child's Autism Risk Accelerates with Mother's Age Over 30," April 22, 2014, http://drexel.edu/ now/archive/2014/April/Autism-Risk-Older-Parents/.
2. Emily Pearle Kingsley, "Welcome to Holland."
3. Autism Speaks, August 15, 2011, http://www.autismspeaks.org/about-us/ press-releases/study-finds-risk-autism-among-younger-siblings-child-autism -much-greater-pre.
4. Brett S. Abrahams and Daniel H. Geschwind, "Advances in Autism Genetics: On the Threshold of a New Neurobiology," *Nature Reviews Genetics* 9, no. 5 (May 2008): 341–55, http://www.ncbi.nlm.nih.gov/pmc/articles/PMC2756414/.
5. Diane Morca, CBS Channel 58 News, May 18, 2012, http://www.cbs58.com/ news/local-news/Waukesha-water-tainted-nearly-half-of-last-year-151995885.html.
6. See "How to Talk about Autism," National Autistic Society, http://www. autism.org.uk/news-and-events/media-centre/how-to-talk-about-autism.aspx.

Chapter 5 I Get Paid for This, Right?

1. Jacques Steinberg, "Savage Stands by Autism Remarks," *New York Times*, July 22, 2008, http://www.nytimes.com/2008/07/22/business/media/22sava. html?_r=1.

2. According to the National Autism Association, nearly half of children with an ASD will wander or elope from a safe environment at some point (http:// nationalautismassociation.org/resources/autism-safety-facts/). So compelling is this tendency that the AAWARE initiative was launched by six nonprofit autism organizations in an attempt to prevent autism-related wandering incidents and deaths (www.aaware.org). The mortality rate for those with autism is twice that of the general population, with drowning the number one cause of accidental death.

Chapter 7 Fortune Favors Anyone but Me

1. Arthur Bisbane, "William Henry Channing's Symphony," editorial from the Hearst newspapers, ca. 1920.

Chapter 9 Mind Control and Major Mom

1. Alinda Gillott, Fred Furniss, and Ann Walter, "Anxiety in High-Functioning Children with Autism," *Autism 5*, no. 3 (September 2001): 277–86, http://aut. sagepub.com/content/5/3/277.short.

2. See "Depression and Anxiety in Patients with Behçet's Disease Compared with That in Patients with Psoriasis" (abstract), *International Journal of Dermatology* 46 (11):1118–24. http://www.ncbi.nlm.nih.gov/pubmed/17988328, accessed Oct. 21, 2004; and "The Relationship between Disease Activity and Depression in Patients with Behcet Disease and Rheumatoid Arthritis" (abstract), *Rheumatology International* 30 (7):941–6. doi: 10.1007/s00296-009-1080-7. Epub 2009 Aug 6. http://www.ncbi.nlm.nih.gov/pubmed/19657642, accessed Oct. 21, 2014.

3. Greg O'Brien, "Suffering at the Hands of the Black Dog," *Huffington Post*, Sept. 8, 2014, huffingtonpost.com/greg-obrien.

4. National Alliance on Mental Illness, "Winston Churchill and His 'Black Dog' That Helped Win World War II," http://www.nami.org/Content/NavigationMenu/ Not_Alone/Winston_Churchill.htm, accessed April 18, 2014.

5. National Institute of Mental Health, "Neuroimaging and Mental Illness: A Window into the Brain," http://www.nimh.nih.gov/health/publications/neuro imaging-and-mental-illness-a-window-into-the-brain/index.shtml, accessed April 18, 2014.

Sarah Parshall Perry is a wife and mother of three children ages ten and under. She has a BS in journalism and a JD from the University of Virginia School of Law, and serves as Senior Fellow at the Family Research Council in Washington DC. Sarah coauthored *When the Fairy Dust Settles: A Mother and Her Daughter Discuss What Really Matters* (New York: FaithWords, 2004) with her mother, Janet Parshall; is a contributor to three blogs; and is the author of numerous magazine articles and award-winning short stories. Sarah has served in youth ministry for over ten years and writes for www.ChosenFamilies.org where she uses her sons' autism spectrum diagnoses to encourage other families living with disabilities. She lives in Baltimore, Maryland, with her husband, her three children, and way too many animals.

VISIT

SarahPerryWrites.com

TO LEARN MORE

OTHER BOOKS
YOU MAY ENJOY

I AM IN HERE

The inspiring personal
journey of a mother
and her non-verbal
daughter with autism
who found a creative
way to break through
the silence and offer
the world an inside
look at the mind of
an autistic child.

SURVIVING HENRY

The heartwarming,
laugh-out-loud story
of a disaster-prone
dog who taught his
family what really
matters in life.

CHOOSING TO SEE

The wife of Steven
Curtis Chapman
shares about the loss
of her daughter, the
struggle to heal, and
the unexpected path
God has placed her on.
Includes a 16-page full
color photo insert.